THE HOLY SPIRIT

Handley Moule

Christian Heritage

Christian Focus Publications publishes biblically-accurate books for adults and children. The books in the adult range are published in three imprints.

Christian Heritage contains classic writings from the past.

Christian Focus contains popular works including biographies, commentaries, doctrine, and Christian living.

Mentor focuses on books written at a level suitable for Bible College and seminary students, pastors, and others; the imprint includes commentaries, doctrinal studies, examination of current issues, and church history.

For a free catalogue of all our titles, please write to
Christian Focus Publications,
Geanies House, Fearn,
Ross-shire, IV20 1TW, Great Britain

For details of our titles visit us on our web site
http://www.christianfocus.com

Originally published in 1890 as *Veni Creator: Thoughts on the person and work of the Holy Spirit of promise*. Most of the footnotes in the previous editions have been omitted from this edition. A small number of editorial changes have also been made.

Published in 1999
by
Christian Focus Publications,
Geanies House, Fearn, Ross-shire,
IV20 1TW, Great Britain.

Contents

PREFACE

The subject of the following chapters needs no prefatory introduction to the Christian reader. In itself eternally and divinely important, it has become in the mercy of God a special subject of our own time. Far and wide in the Christian church, amidst too many phenomena of peril and perplexity, we hail as a phenomenon of good and glorious omen an ever-deepening attention to the divine promises which gather round the truth of the Holy Ghost. More and ever more it is recognised by those who name the Name of the *Son* that, alike for individual blessing and for the work and witness of the Community, we depend with an absolute need upon the presence and power of the *Spirit*.

May these pages, for all their fragmentary character, be used in some measure by *him* of whom they speak to stir up his saints so always to lay hold on him that he evermore may lay hold on them, and graciously fill them with himself.

Cambridge,
March 28th, 1890.

Chapter 1

The Personality of the Holy Spirit

The following chapters have a very simple purpose. They are not intended to constitute a technical treatise, certainly not to carry the reader into elaborate enquiries into the history of doctrines. They are intended to be a reverent review of some, and only some, of the main teachings of the Holy Scriptures, concerning the ever-blessed Spirit of God, the heavenly Paraclete, the eternal third person, the Lord and life-giver, and his revealed work in redemption. And this review shall be made, by his most merciful assistance, with a constant reference to the actual needs of the human soul, the actual experience of the people of God.

The theme is one of altogether special importance for the believing church of these latter days. In John Owen's *Pneumatologia*, his deep, massive and most spiritual 'Discourse Concerning the Holy Spirit' (1674), occurs a remarkable passage (bk. 1, ch. 1), in which he traces through the ages and dispensations a certain progress of divine tests of living orthodoxy, related to each of the three persons in succession. Before the first advent the great testing truth was 'the oneness of God's nature and his monarchy over all', with special respect to the person of the Father. At the first advent the great question was whether a church orthodox on the first point would now receive the divine Son, incarnate, sacrificed and glorified, according to the promise. And when the working of this test had gathered out the church of Christian believers,

7

and built it on the foundation of the truth of the person
and work of the Lord Jesus Christ, then the Holy Spirit
came in a new prominence and speciality before that
church as a touchstone of true faith.

> 'Wherefore the duty of the church now immediately respects
> the Spirit of God, who acts towards it in the name of the
> Father and of the Son; and with respect unto him it is that
> the church in its present state is capable of an apostasy from
> God.... The sin of despising his person and rejecting his work
> now is of the same nature with idolatry of old, and the Jews'
> rejection of the person of the Son.'

The statement is perhaps too absolute in form to embrace
all the data of revelation and experience. But it is at least
an indication of great spiritual facts, and a solemn caution
to the Christian of the present day to take heed lest he lose
hold of the truth of the blessed Spirit in its humbling but
beautifying fulness. All too easily, amidst prevalent fashions
of opinion in the modern church, we may insensibly,
unconsciously, let that truth fall from us. We may take up
with a view of human nature in its fallen estate which shall
practically dispense with the need of the regenerating and
sanctifying Holy Ghost. We may take up with a view of
sacred order and divine ordinances which shall in effect
put his sovereign and mysterious work into other hands
than his. May he, the Lord, the life-giver, personal,
sovereign, loving, mighty, preserve us from unfaithfulness
of regard towards his blessed person, from untruth of view
of his divine work. May he keep us indeed 'men of the
Spirit', filling us, that we may be so, with himself.

As we approach our subject more immediately, let us
very deliberately take the attitude of invocation and

adoration. Who can rightly think and discourse about the Holy Spirit of God save by that same Spirit, and as seeking with humblest reverence to follow the very syllables and footsteps of that written Word which has him everywhere for its true Author?

It is recorded in the story of the German Reformation that on one of its most memorable occasions, the disputation between Eck and Luther before Duke George of Saxony at the castle of the Pleissenburg, the controversy was preluded by the solemn chant of the *Veni Creator*, sung thrice over while the whole assembly knelt. With the voices of the soul may we, writer and reader, so now unite, as we approach not a great battle of arguments but a series of quiet meditations upon the person and the work of the Lord the Spirit.

> 'Veni, Creator Spiritus,
> Mentes Tuorum visita;
> Imple superna gratia
> Quae Tu creasti pectora;
>
> 'Qui Paraclitus diceris,
> Altissimi donum Dei,
> Fons vivus, Ignis, Caritas,
> Et spiritalis Unctio.'[1]

---

1. 'Come, Holy Ghost, Creator, come,
      And visit all the souls of Thine;
   Thou hast inspired our hearts with life,
      Inspire them now with life divine.

   'Thou art the Comforter, the Gift
      Of God most High, the Fire of love,
   The everlasting Spring of joy,
      And holy Unction from above.'

In the present chapter I propose to speak of the revealed *personality* of the Holy Spirit as the all-important preliminary to all other thoughts concerning him. Upon his divinity, his deity, there is little practical need that I should dwell, so plain it is on the very surface of Scripture that the Holy Spirit, whether personal or not, is divine, is a Power of the divine Order. But is it *he*, or *it*? Is it a divine faculty, influence, phase, mode, or a divine person?

Now the most direct answer to this question, and at the same time the deepest and tenderest, is to go at once to the central passage of all Scripture in the matter. All over the blessed Book, from its very first lines onward, lie scattered mentions of the Spirit and his work. Here and there we have passages which go almost the length of revealing explicitly his personality; here and there passages which fully go that length, fairly interpreted. But there is one precious section of Scripture which is to these scattered rays as their combining focus, the glorious ruling passage of the subject. And where and what is it? Not some great chapter of apostolic argument and exposition, such as those in which the Godhead of the Son is asserted, or the holy paradox of justification by faith explained and applied to the trembling, weary conscience and longing heart. No; for the decisive teaching on the personality of the Holy Ghost we go yet deeper into the Scripture tabernacle; we enter its Holiest; we open the pages where the Lord Jesus himself teaches with his own lips the secrets of spiritual life. There, as it were under the Shekinah itself, lies our doctrinal stronghold for this article of faith (John 14–16). There speaks the Christ of God, in an hour of supreme tenderness, and from which all ideas of the rhetorical and the merely poetical are infinitely distant; and he speaks with repetition and emphasis of this same Holy Spirit, and he speaks of him as personal. My readers are well aware of the fact. But it is never in vain to impress such a fact again upon the soul by re-examination of the infallible words. Let me ask that the Greek be once more opened, and this divine grammatical anomaly once more studied – the neuter $\pi\nu\epsilon\upsilon\mu\alpha^2$ associated repeatedly and markedly with the masculine $\pi\alpha\rho\alpha\kappa\lambda\eta\tau o\varsigma^3$, the masculines $\acute{o}\varsigma$, $\acute{\epsilon}\kappa\epsilon\iota\nu o\varsigma$, $\alpha\acute{\upsilon}\tau o\varsigma^4$ (John 14:16, 17; 15:26; 16:7, 8). And let this be read in the light of the wonderful context, in which this blessed *Paraclete,* this *Advocatus,* 'called in' to the aid of the otherwise 'orphaned' church, is seen to be such, and to act so, as to be indeed the Substitute, the more than substitute, for the unspeakably real personality of the Saviour in his seen presence. The passage sets the Holy Spirit before us as not the Father, as not the Son, and yet as the 'Vicar of Christ' (the phrase is Tertullian's), the ample Consolation for the absence of the familiar company of the beloved Saviour. It scarcely needs the impressive testimony of the Greek grammar of the sentences to assure us with deep and restful certainty that to the mind of the Saviour that night the Spirit was indeed present as a person.

In this central and decisive passage then we have the

---

2. *Pneuma*: Wind – Spirit – A spirit – Spiritual being – One's soul in Spirit.

3. *Parakletos*: 'Called to one's aid' in a court of justice. A defender.

4. And if the question is asked, what language did the Lord Jesus speak that night, Greek or Aramaic; and if Aramaic, how was the contrast between masculine and neuter conveyed? We reply that the question, most interesting and important in itself, is not in point in our enquiry. For us as believers in the divine character of the written Word the discourses of the New Testament, and of the Old Testament too, are before us as *reports corrected and edited by the Author.*

Holy Ghost revealed to us in so many words as *him*, not
only as *it*; as the living and conscious exerciser of true
personal will and love, as truly and fully as the first
'Paraclete' (1 John 2:1), the Lord Jesus Christ himself.
And now this central passage radiates out its glory upon
the whole system and circle of Scripture truth about the
Spirit. From Genesis 1:2 to Revelation 22:17, it sheds the
warmth of divine personal life into every mention of the
blessed Power.[5] With the Paschal Discourse in our heart
and mind, we know that it was he, not it, who 'brooded
over the primeval deep (Gen. 1:2). He, not it, 'strove with
man', or 'ruled in man' of old (Gen. 6:3). He, not it, was
in Joseph in Egypt (Gen. 41:38), and upon Moses in the
wilderness of wandering (Num. 11:17), and upon judges
and kings of after-days. He, not it, 'spake by the prophets,'
'moving' those 'holy men of God' (Judg. 6:34; 1 Sam.
10:10). He, not it, drew the plan of the ancient Tabernacle
and of the first Temple (1 Sam. 22:2; 2 Kgs. 2:9, 15; 2
Chron. 15:1; Matt. 22:43; Heb. 10:15; 1 Pet. 1:11; 2 Pet.
1:21; Heb. 9:8; 1 Chron. 28:12). He, not it, lifted Ezekiel
to his feet in the hour of vision (Ezek. 2:2). He, not it,
came upon the Virgin (Luke 1:35), and anointed her Son
at Jordan (Luke 3:22) and led him to the desert of
temptation (Luke 4:1), and gave utterances to the saints at

5. I well know that it is maintained that in the Greek New Testament,
as a rule, τo $\Pi\nu\epsilon\upsilon\mu\alpha$ denotes the Personal Paraclete, and $\pi\nu\epsilon\upsilon\mu\alpha$
with the article not the person, but the influence. With some exceptions
I believe this rule holds good. But it leaves quite untouched the line
of reasoning in the text here. When we have ascertained that τo
$\Pi\nu\epsilon\upsilon\mu\alpha$ is indeed a person we know that $\pi\nu\epsilon\upsilon\mu\alpha$ is a *personal
influence*. And in the general light of Scripture teaching on divine
Influences we are abundantly secure in saying that this means nothing
less than *the divine person at work*.

Pentecost (Acts 2:4), and caught Philip away from the road to Gaza (Acts 8:39), and guided Paul through Asia Minor to the nearest port for Europe (Acts 16:6, 7). He, not it, effects the new birth of regenerate man (John 3:5, 6, 8), and is the breath of his new life (Gal. 5:25), and the earnest of his coming glory (Rom. 8:11; Eph. 1:13, 14). By him, not it, the believer walks (Gal. 5:25), and mortifies the deeds of the body (Rom. 8:13), filled not with it, but him (Eph. 5:18). He, not it, is the Spirit of faith (2 Cor. 4:13), by whom it is 'given unto us to believe on Christ' (Phil. 1:29). He, not it, speaks to the Churches (Rev. 2:7, 11, 29; 3:6, 13, 22). He, not it, says from heaven that they who die in the Lord are blessed, and calls in this life (Rev. 14:13) upon the wandering soul of man to come to the living water (Rev. 22:17).

And let us not wonder, by the way, that the exhibition of his personality is comparatively so reserved in Scripture; that we have need, as in the case of the personality of the Father and of the Son we have not at all, to place Scripture by Scripture and make an induction on the subject. The reason lies in the nature of the case. The Holy Spirit is the true author of the written Word; and his authorship there is occupied with the main and absorbing theme not of himself but of another person, the Son of God (Heb. 10:15). Incidentally, like some of his human agents in the production of the Scriptures – like Moses, and Jeremiah, and Paul, and John – he discloses enough of his blessed self to give us full apprehension of his personal reality; but his theme, his burden, is *Jesus Christ*. And again in the unfolding and application of redemption, his work is above all things secret, internal, subjective. It is to take of the things of Christ, to deal with the blessed objectivity of

the finished work and inexhaustible riches of Christ, and
with inmost touches and new-creating whispers to manifest
them to the spirit of man. It is to bring man, by a divine
but inscrutable operation, to believe in Christ and to
possess him, with a spontaneity truly man's own while
yet another is in it. As to his saving operations, the Spirit
lies hidden as it were behind Christ Jesus and in our own
inner man. So it is also in measure in his revelations of
himself in his holy Word.

However, this by the way. The point before us now, in
the matter of the personality of the Spirit, is just this: that
we have the central and open revelation of that personality
given us in Scripture in a place and under circumstances
charged with indescribable tenderness and sacredness. The
truth thus appears not only as a demand on the obedience
of faith – though this it is indeed – but as a gift to the
believing soul of heavenly love, of love deep and warm as
the heart of the Redeemer.

There seems to be a drift and set at the present day, in
many quarters where what are called liberalizing
tendencies in theology prevail, to discredit, or minimize,
or ignore, the belief of the personality of the blessed Spirit.
In what interest and to what end, one asks, is such a
tendency accepted or promoted? Surely not with the hope
of presenting the Christian plan, the process of eternal love
and goodness, in fairer, tenderer, or more living colours
and glories. If a reference to personal experience may be
permitted I may indeed here 'set to my seal'. Never shall
I forget the gain to conscious faith and peace which came
to my own soul, not long after a first decisive and
appropriating view of the crucified Lord as the sinner's
sacrifice of peace, from a more intelligent and conscious

hold upon the living and most gracious personality of that Holy Spirit through whose mercy the soul had got that blessed view. It was a new development of insight into the love of God. It was a new contact, as it were, with the inner and eternal movements of redeeming goodness and power, a new discovery in divine resources. At such a 'time of finding', gratitude and love and adoration gain a new, a newly realized, reason, and motive-power and rest. He who with his secret skill, and with a power not the less almighty because it violates nothing, has awakened and regenerated the man, now shines before his inner sight with the smile of a personal and eternal kindness and amity, and is seen standing side by side, in union unspeakable yet without confusion, with him who has suffered and redeemed, and with him who laid the mighty plan of grace, and willed its all-merciful success, and spared not his own Son, giving him over for us all. If I may reverently use the simile, it is as when to two notes of the musical triad the related third note is added, and there results, in the words of the music-loving poet, 'not a fourth sound, but a star.'[9]

As our enquiry proceeds we shall have continual occasion of course to recur to this primary theme, the personality of the Holy Ghost; and much that has been omitted in this preliminary statement will thus be supplied. But we have at least aimed here at the great mark of setting the sacred fact, as a fact, well before us, and letting it take its large place anew in the consciousness, and so in the action, of the believing man. That place is surely meant to be a large one, in the light of the Paschal Discourse, as we have traced its import. There the blessed person of the Paraclete is revealed as just about to fill the void of the

6. Browning, *Abt Vogler.*

disciples' hearts with a whole wealth of personal, gracious action, abiding, revealing, teaching, leading, conveying into the inmost receptacle the presence of Christ, so that he while absent should be present, while invisible should be seen. Surely such a presence and such an action was intended to call forth on the happy Christian's part a reverent and loving reciprocation. If thus the Spirit was to deal with him, he was to deal with the Spirit in holy recognition, and adoring gratitude, and confiding love. 'The Spirit with our spirit' (Rom. 8:16) is a phrase meant to carry endless blessed applications in the experiences of the life of faith.

As we close, the question perhaps arises from the thoughts just suggested, whether acts of direct adoration to the Holy Spirit are prescribed to us in the Scriptures. It is certainly remarkable that we have very little in their pages which bears explicitly on the question, a fact which however falls very naturally in with what we have already seen of the general comparative reticence of the author of the Book about his own nature and glory. And, again, it is a fact in harmony with what we have seen of the character of his work for the Christian; a work pre-eminently subjective, so profoundly so as to occasion such a statement as that of Paul that the Spirit intercedes for the saints with groanings that cannot be uttered (Rom. 8:27), words whose context at least suggests that the intercession has its action in the region of the inner man, and breathes itself or groans itself forth through the regenerate human spirit. If it is the Holy Spirit's special function not only to speak to and deal with, but also to speak and work through, the man he renews and sanctifies, we can just so far understand that he the less presents himself for our articulate adoration.

But meanwhile the sacred rightfulness of our worship of the Holy Spirit is as surely established as anything can be that rests on large and immediate inferences from the Scriptures. If he is divine, and if he is personal, how can we help the attitude of adoration when, leaving for the moment the thought of his work in us, we isolate in our view the thought of him the Worker? Scripture practically prescribes to us such an attitude when it gives us our Lord's own account, in his baptismal formula, of the eternal *name* as his disciples were to know it – 'The name of the Father, and of the Son, and of the Holy Ghost'; and when in the Acts and Epistles the Holy Ghost is set before us as not only doing his work in the inmost being of the individual but presiding in sacred majesty over the community; and when in the Revelation he, in the mystical sevenfoldness of his operation (Acts 5:3; Acts 13:2; Acts 15:28; 1 Cor. 12:11-13), Seven yet One, appears in that solemn prelude as the concurrent Giver, with the Father and the Son, of grace and peace; above all when in the Paschal Discourse (Rev. 1:4; John 14:16) the adorable and adored Lord Jesus presents him to our faith as co-ordinate with himself in glory and grace, 'another Comforter'.

So, while watchfully and reverently seeking to remember the laws of Scripture proportion, and that according to it the believer's relation to the Spirit is *not so much* that of direct adoration as of a reliance which wholly implies it, let us trustfully and thankfully worship him, and ask blessing of him, as our spirits shall be moved to such action under his grace. Let us ever and again recollect, with deliberate contemplation and faith, what by his Word we know of him, and of his presence in us and his work for us, and then let us not only 'pray *in* the Holy Ghost'

(Jude 20) but also *to* him, whether in the words of some
ancient *Veni*, or in the many songs of supplication which
have been given us, surely not without his leading, in these
latter days of his gracious dispensation. One such out of
many let me quote and let me use, breathed from the soul
and mind of my own beloved and Spirit-taught father long
ago, and sung by him (how often! in tones how well
remembered!) in his hours of adoration to the last:

> 'Come, Holy Comforter, celestial Light,
> Relieve from all obscurity our sight;
> Come, Holy Comforter, celestial Fire,
> Our souls with love and purity inspire;
> Hear, Holy Ghost, our supplicating cry,
> Nor leave the grace Thou gav'st to droop and die.

> 'Come, Holy Comforter, a Saviour's love
> Reveal, and fix our hearts on joys above;
> Come, Holy Comforter, the flesh subdue,
> And aid us, one with Christ, his will to do;
> Hear, Holy Ghost, our supplicating cry,
> Nor leave the grace Thou gav'st to droop and die.'

Addendum to Chapter 1

The Sin of Railing ($\beta\lambda\alpha\sigma\phi\eta\mu\iota\alpha$)
Against the Holy Ghost

(Matt. 12:31, 32; Mark 3:28-30; Luke 12:10.
See Heb. 6:4-8, 10:26-31; 1 John 5:16.)

On this awful and mysterious subject I offer only a very
few words, and these are offered mainly because of the

connection of the subject with that of the personality of the Holy Spirit. For it appears to be justly reckoned among the proofs of the personality that this unspeakably dread warning should be given, in which railing against the Spirit is seen as a sin comparable in kind with railing against the holy personal Saviour.

For myself I feel, as surely many a Christian does, how very much easier it is to say what this great acme and last development of sin *is not* than what it is. Whatever it is, it is always and for ever true that the man who as a fact comes penitent to the feet of Christ for pardon finds it. And whatever it is, the Saviour's own words of warning surely imply that it is not, so to speak, a terrible accident of the sinful soul's action but a development, the result of a process, the outcome of a deliberately formed condition. In order to it there needs, assuredly, the concurrence of great and God-given *light* upon good and evil, sin and salvation (see Heb. 6), with a resolved, deliberate and matured hostility and repulsion on the part of the will; a personal hatred of recognized eternal holiness.

Why is this sin unpardonable? Because, surely, it is such a closing of the door of repentance by the created personality against itself as, by laws of spiritual nature which we cannot analyse but may in part divine, shuts up the personality finally against grace; denies all possible ground, all *nidus*, to the action of him who it has in some sense seen and yet deliberately hated. And some further light, if I mistake not, is thrown on this *irremissibility* by the fact that the gospel, the dispensation of the Spirit (see e.g. 2 Cor. 3:6-8), is seen in Scripture as the *final* message of divine mercy. He who in the full light of this final gospel deliberately rejects its message and its messenger, casts off the *last* offers, the justly and necessarily last, of salvation. No *more* powerful, tender, prevailing secrets of conquest and persuasion lie beyond. This comes out in Hebrews 10, where the possible apostate, back from Christ to antichristian Judaism, is warned that no new sacrifice for sin will meet his awful need. The old offerings have done their work for ever; and Calvary will not be repeated. From one point of view we may thus say that the warnings of the Saviour in the Gospels mean, in effect, that while a merciful forbearance could, in the nature of things, be extended for his sake to that rejection of him which was committed 'in the days of his flesh', while he stood before his enemies as pre-eminently 'The Son of *Man*', it would be otherwise when he was deliberately and finally refused under the dispensation of that Holy Spirit who should bear witness to him in his accomplished work and glory as 'the captain of salvation made perfect'.

Can the truly regenerate commit this sin? I venture to say *yes* and *no*. In themselves, and as relying more on their regeneration than their regenerator, *yes*. In him, and under his covenant of grace, I humbly believe, *no and never*. Hebrews 6:4-8, as it appears to me, deals with the case not of the soul vivified with the divine life of holiness and love by the Spirit of Christ, but of the soul gifted by that Spirit with the fullest *light, separable from love*. Balaam's recorded condition remarkably illustrates every detail of Hebrews 6:4-8.

Meanwhile let us take heed, watching and praying, not to grieve the Spirit of love and holiness. It is better to be dismayed than to presume. But it is best of all most reverently to trust.

Chapter 2

(a) Procession of the Spirit

(b) Work of the Spirit in relation to the human nature of our Lord Jesus Christ

Veni Creator Spiritus was the thought with which our previous chapter closed. Let us begin again with the same. In following the scriptural traces of the doctrine of the blessed Spirit we will remember that he is the promised 'guide into all the truth' (John 16:13). By him we will seek 'a right judgment in all things' concerning his revealed glory, such a judgment that we may 'evermore rejoice in his holy comfort', the comfort of a happy insight into what he is as Comforter.

I propose to treat in this chapter of two important sides of the doctrine of the Spirit; the forthcoming of the Spirit in the Holy Trinity from the Father and the Son ('the Dual Procession'), and the work of the Spirit in relation to the human nature of our Lord Jesus Christ.

1. The words *procession of the Spirit* can scarcely be spoken or written without calling up associated thoughts and strife and division within the Christian church, and the hardly less unhappy remembrance of that ultra-speculative treatment of divine truths which has too often proved a fruitful source of divisions. Not seldom even the most pious and reverent minds have been beguiled into discussing the nature of God and the eternal relations of

the divine Persons in a tone which would be justified only if we had actually 'found out the Almighty unto perfection' (Job 11:7) and saw before us, arranged in a series of absolutely certain premises, major and minor, all that *he* knows about *himself*. Hence in no small measure arose that great controversy of East and West upon the dual procession which led to a final rupture about the year 1050, a rupture never since healed, nay so little healed that as recently as 1863 a declaration was issued from Constantinople condemning as heresy the Western belief, confessed in our two longer Creeds and in the Fifth Anglican Article.

But notwithstanding all this it is fully possible, I trust, to treat this subject of the dual procession, great and also tender as it is, without either a long discussion of the history of belief or an unconscious imitation of the speculative tendency referred to. All I ask now to do is to take this doctrine, which our church, both before and after the Reformation, has as a fact avowed to be Scripture truth, and to look upon it in the serene and blessed light of the revealed and experienced work of the Lord, the life-giver, in his ministry for Christ in the church and the soul. We shall surely find it to be no mere phantom of abstract and unlicensed speculation, but a truth of life and love.

What then in effect do we mean when we speak of the procession of the Spirit from the Father and the Son? We mean that in the revealed inner relations of Godhead, in those eternal and necessary relations, 'necessary' in the well-understood sense that they are relations lying in the very nature of God, relations which in that nature *must be*, even as holiness *must be* in it), while the Father is the eternal origin of the eternal Spirit, the Son is concurrently his eternal origin also. We mean that Godhead is eternally in the Spirit because of the Son as well as because of the Father. We do not mean that the blessed Son is thus the Spirit's origin in an independent and separated way. *All* that the Son is, as the second person of the Holy Trinity, he is 'of the Father', and of the Father alone. To this he bore abundant personal witness 'in the days of his flesh' (John 5:25, etc.). But we believe that the 'all' which he thus eternally derives includes *inter alia* this – that he is, with the Father, the concurrent origin of the Holy Spirit.

Such a humble belief is neither an arbitrary and barren demand upon a bewildered or unreflecting assent, nor a thing so sublimated and vanishing as to find no point of contact with life and love. In the first place, it throws some precious light of its own upon that *Sanctum Santorum* of life and love, the inner relations of the persons of the blessed Godhead. He who is at once the Spirit of the Father and the Spirit of the Son, and one with both – is he not, in his blessed personal existence, the result, the bond, the vehicle, of their everlasting mutual delight and love? That such he is was the belief of Christians long ago, a belief resting not indeed upon direct revelation, but upon inferences deep and lawful suggested by it. It is put into articulate statements by Augustine, in his treatise *On the Trinity*, 6:5. It falls in with the doctrine of the dual procession in a true harmony. And surely the study of anything which casts light on the revelation of that mutual love is full of practical blessing to thoughtful faith, for it is a contribution to the study of that inexhaustible text, '*God is love*' (1 John 4:8, 16). Yes, not only does God do acts of love, however great. In the inmost heart and secret of his being he '*is love*'.

And when we come from the revealed inner life of Godhead to the divine works of redemption, we find a manifest aid and blessing in the belief of the eternal forthcoming of the Holy Spirit from the Son as well as from the Father. In the light of this belief, every part and detail of the work of the Spirit in connection with the person and work of Christ gains indefinitely in our view in respect of closeness and tenderness of contact. In the light of this belief, he who 'testifies of' Christ, and 'glorifies' him, and imparts him, does all this blessed work not only as the holy messenger and co-operator of the Saviour but as the stream from him the fountain. Deep must be the harmonies of such co-operation. Absolute must be the truth and fulness of such testimony. Close, unspeakably close, must be the union effected by such an intermediary.

Meanwhile the scriptural basis for this belief is strong, and capable of simple statement. In Scripture the Spirit is as freely called 'the Spirit of the Son' (Gal. 4: 6), 'the Spirit of Christ' (Rom. 8:9; 1 Pet. 1:11), as the 'Spirit of God' (Eph. 3:16), 'the Spirit of the Father' (Luke 24:49). And he is as freely said to be 'sent' by the Son as by the Father. But we gather from Scripture, with abundant fulness, and in many directions, that the works of the blessed three persons in redemption bear always a deep and steadfast reference to their eternal inner relations. Thus the eternal Father of the Son, and not the Son, is the Father of the believer. The eternal Son, and not the Father, is the firstborn among many brethren. Therefore, by the rule of a deep and holy analogy, we believe that the relation of the Spirit to the Son in respect of saving work rests upon their relation in respect of eternal being. Him who is 'the

Spirit of the Son, sent by the Son', for us men and for our salvation, we humbly and adoringly believe to be related to the Son in the inner sanctuary of Godhead after the manner of an unbeginning and unending procession, forthcoming of divine life.

If such is indeed the truth, let our insight into it rise higher, infinitely higher, than any mere analysis or record, however careful, of a great church controversy. It is a thing which can and should lead us up to look upon the very springs of life eternal. It is one of the mighty truths which converge upon the inexhaustible glory and precious-ness of our Lord Jesus Christ; upon his central position for us in the plan of salvation; upon the close connection with him, the infinitely close connection, of all parts of that plan and work; the parts which concern our holiness as truly as these which concern our acceptance.

2. This last thought leads me to a few considerations on our second present topic; the work of the Holy Spirit in relation to the human nature of our Lord Jesus Christ. On this topic I dwell in order above all to emphasize some practical spiritual truths about the Spirit's regenerating and sanctifying work for us who come to Christ and are in him.

It is but rapidly, and as collecting specimens of illustration, that I need remind my readers of the large and deep connection revealed in Scripture between the Holy Spirit and the *Son of Man*.

The Holy Spirit was the immediate agent in the immaculate conception of 'that holy thing' (Luke 1:35). Not that he was therefore the Father of the blessed Son;

but he was the vehicle of the paternity. Not again that he
so acted that the Son as God had nothing to do with the
act of the incarnation. The Son, in divine will, willed to
assume our nature, and so assumed it; but again the blessed
Spirit wrought the process whereby that will was carried
out. And then, thirty years later, the Spirit descended upon
the youthful Lord at his baptism, in some inscrutable
speciality of presence (Matt. 3:16; etc.) and power (Luke
4:1-14). In this 'power of the Spirit' he went forth first to
temptation and then to ministry. It was in the Spirit, 'given
without measure', that he 'spoke the words of God' (John
3:34). It was 'by means of the eternal Spirit', wonderful
phrase, that he (Heb. 9:14) 'offered himself without spot
to God'. We find indications that the Spirit had great things
to do with the bodily resurrection of the buried Lord (Rom.
8:11). After resurrection it was 'by the Holy Spirit' that
he 'gave commandment to the apostles' (Acts 1:2). And
when in the Revelation the glorified Jesus, as the slain
one risen again and ascended, speaks to the seven
Churches, the voices of the Saviour and of the Spirit are
as one (Rev. 2:1-7, etc.).

With the reserve of humblest reverence, may we not
say that the manhood of our dear Redeemer was produced,
and maintained all along in its absolute perfection, not by
his own action as God the Son but by that of God the Holy
Spirit? His own divine act in the matter was, as we have
said, and as Owen said long ago, to *assume* the manhood,
but no more. Never indeed, not for one moment from the
first, was that manhood dissociated from the godhead of
the Son. Never for a moment had it a personality
independent of that of God the Son. The very person who
said, in the days of his flesh 'Before Abraham was, I am'

(John 8:58), the person who under his great humiliation said to a whole world of sin and sorrow, 'Come unto Me' (Matt. 11:28) was then and there as truly God[1] as he was before the world was. But all this leaves untouched the sacred truth that the manhood he took was, in the divine order and law, manhood begun and maintained in its perfect holiness and power by the Holy Spirit as the immediate personal divine worker. It is accordingly by the Holy Spirit that the Lord Jesus Christ is the second man. It is by the Holy Spirit that he, as the second man now glorified, is the receptacle, the reservoir, the fountain-head, of that 'all fulness' which dwells in him for us (Col. 1:19; 2:9).

We pass almost instantly in the treatment of such a subject into regions beyond our analysis. But we see enough to deepen and strengthen our 'faith in the operation of God' (Col. 2:12) to impart a growing definiteness of

---

1. And not God in abeyance, as some have seemed to say, giving to his *Kenôsis* (Phil. 2:7) a meaning not borne out by Scripture. On the theory that he so 'made himself void' as to become liable to mental error, mistakes of fact and reasoning, for example about the age and nature of the Old Testament Scriptures, see by all means Liddon, *Bampton Lectures*, Lecture 8. It may be enough here to point out that to view such a voluntary fallibility on our Lord's part as an instance of his blessed *self-humiliation* involves a certain confusion of conceptions. It would stand, supposing it to be true, under a very different description from, for instance, his voluntary liability to fatigue, sorrow, and death. A rich and refined philanthropist, bent on elevating a degraded tribe, would give a beautiful instance of self-humiliation in consenting, if it were expedient, to be as poor, and as badly lodged as they. But if, while coming as their teacher, he consented to share their ignorance (were it possible) on matters on which he undertook to teach them, he would deprive himself to their loss and disadvantage.

view, and a fuller peace in the heart, and a more humble
adoration, as we ponder our own transition, by the power
of the Spirit, 'from death unto life', and onwards always
to 'life more abundant' (John 5:24; 10:10).

For in this recollection of the truth of the Spirit's work
on and in the manhood of our blessed Head, we are brought
directly to a fuller recollection also of the *place of Christ*
(if I may express myself so) in the Holy Spirit's saving
work for us. Let us take this up as our closing topic for
this chapter.

We who believe indeed in the Lord Jesus Christ know
on the evidence of God's Word that we owe our saving
faith to the Lord the Spirit, 'the Spirit of faith' (2 Cor.
4:13). We who were once 'dead in trespasses and sins'
(Eph. 2:1), and who now live, know on the same evidence
that we were, in 'abundant mercy', 'born of the Spirit'
(John 3:8), and that every step which we take in that life
we take 'by the Spirit' (Gal. 5:25).

Is the 'sound' of regenerate vitality and action 'heard',
in however small a whisper yet *audibly,* in our souls and
in the outward life which manifests their condition? It is
the blessed Spirit's presence in special grace. It is the
evidence, the one evidence, of our real new birth, new
creation, by him. I say, it is the one evidence of this. For
let us remember that across all the problems of sacramental
operation we must read always those words of our Lord
about the mystic Wind. Wherever that *Wind* is, yes,
wherever it is, by its nature as wind *it moves*; it is not
merely latent; it is heard; 'Thou hearest the sound thereof;
so is every one that is born of the Spirit.' But on this I do
not linger now. Our concern now is with the experiences
of the life of grace in Christ, and their connection with the

personal working of the Spirit. Accordingly, 'in the sanctification of the Spirit' (1 Pet. 1:2), that is to say in his whole work of our separation to God, we were by him (John 16:8) at first brought through conviction 'unto obedience to, and blood-sprinkling of, Jesus Christ' (1 Pet. 1:2). And when the last step of the blessed process shall come, and we shall rise transfigured from the grave, possessing 'the adoption, to wit the redemption of our body' (Rom. 8:23), it will still and forever be 'because of the Spirit who dwelleth in us' (Rom. 8:11). Between this Alpha and this Omega of our personal salvation all is of 'the same Spirit'.

Does the peaceful power of grace pervade our regenerate being, and claim effectually for our Lord all we are and all we have, and bring, spirit, soul and body into a delightful captivity and bondservice to our head and possessor? It is 'the fulness of the Spirit' (Eph. 5:18). Do we day by day 'mortify the deeds of the body'? It is 'by the Spirit' (Rom. 8:13). Do we in truth breathe 'the Abba, that prayer of faith alone'? It is the Spirit, the Spirit of adoption, the Spirit of God's Son in our hearts (Rom. 8:15, 17; Gal. 4:6). Do we pray in truth the prayer of holy faith and love, the prayer that asks according to his will? It is 'in the Holy Ghost' (Jude 20) it is 'the Spirit making intercession for us with groanings that cannot be uttered' (Rom. 8:26). Do 'we wait by faith for the hope of righteousness' (Gal. 5:5), the glory reserved for the justified? It is 'by the Spirit'. Does 'Christ dwell in our hearts by faith?' It is because the Spirit has 'strengthened us with might in our inner man' (Eph. 3:16).

Am I needlessly dwelling upon truths which are, thanks be to God, our most familiar friends among the treasures

of the gospel? It is not wholly for argument that I do so.
To me, there seems to lie in the very recitation of our creed
of the hidden life, a charm and power which the Spirit
himself can wonderfully employ to revive or to develop
in the soul the realization and the use of the precious things
which are in some respects so familiar.

But I come now to what was my main reason for this
review of some of the blessings given to us by the Lord,
the life-giver. I come to say something of the place of
Christ in the Spirit's work.

And here for the present I will speak not only briefly
but in one direction alone. I will not dwell upon the all-
beloved truth of the propitiating cross, and upon the Spirit's
witness to it in our awakened hearts. I will not dwell at all
indeed upon the Spirit's *witness* to the Lord Jesus Christ.
I look at present in the direction only of our UNION with
Jesus Christ in new birth and life by the Spirit.

The Spirit, as our Communion Creed confesses, is the
life-giver, the maker-alive.[2] But what is the *life* which he
gives, with which he works? I listen, and I hear another
voice, which is yet as if also his; and it says, 'I am the life'
(John 11:25; 14:6). 'The life eternal is in the Son'; 'he
that hath the Son hath Life' (1 John 5:12). I read these
great, these blessed words, in the light of what we have
collected now of the Holy Spirit's work on and in the holy
Son of Man; and I thus see in them a remembrance that
what the Spirit does in his free and all-powerful work in
the soul which he quickens into second life is, above all
things, to bring it into contact with the Son. He roots it, he
grafts it, he embodies it, into the Son. He deals so with it
that there is a continuity wholly spiritual indeed but none

2. *Το Ζωοποιον*

the less most real, unfigurative, and efficacious, between the Head and the limb, between the branch and the Root. He effects an influx into the regenerate man of the blessed virtues of the nature of the Second Adam, an infusion of the exalted life of Jesus Christ, through an open duct, living, and divine, into the man who is born again into him the incarnate and glorified Son of God. I see on the one hand the blessed Spirit poured without measure upon the Head. I see him on the other hand, not independently of that Head but in deepest relation to him and union with him, pouring himself richly into the member. I see him the divine Factor in the becoming and being of the manhood of the second Adam. I see him equally the divine factor in the new creation of the sinner into a true child of God, a true and regenerate member of the new race.

And all this combines to remind me that the blessed process all the while has Jesus Christ for its inmost secret. What does the holy life-giver impart, infuse, develop? What is my life eternal in the last analysis? Not himself, the blessed worker and conveyer, but my incarnate, sacrificed and glorified Redeemer and Head. The Spirit pours into me *him*, to be my eternal life for deliverance, for victory, for peace, for service, as truly as he, the same Saviour, is my pardon and righteousness in his once-wrought propitiation.

The life-giver is the giver of Christ who is our life.

'Deep through the springs of mind and soul
    Thee the great Comforter inspires;
Thy sovereign thoughts our thoughts control,
    Thy love our love divinely fires.'

We live in the time when every fundamental of the old and blessed gospel is too often denied, or disparaged, or minimized, even by commissioned ministers of the Word, in favour of something alleged to be more large, and loving and living. Let us not be moved. Let us not 'drift away' (Heb. 2:1) with the stream. Let us not, for lack of taking heed, for lack, above all, of taking heed in secret *for ourselves,* go away with the multitude (John 6:66, 67). But meanwhile let our steadfastness and persistence manifest itself never in *mere* negatives of rebuke or caution, but more and more in the presentation of our glorious positive. In the tranquil power of the giver of light and life let us evermore bring into our faith and into our teaching that blessed fulness of the truth as it is in Jesus, which is nowhere found more certainly than when we view in their harmony, and use them as we view them, those twin treasures of the old unique gospel – the saving work of him who is the one life, and the saving work of him who is the one life-giver.

Chapter 3

The Holy Spirit's Work in Relation to the Holy Scriptures

Thus far we have dealt almost exclusively with the revealed truth of the blessed Spirit's personality and divine glory, only turning aside to remember that most sacred and wonderful of all his works, his action in the Incarnation of the Lord Jesus Christ and in the human life of the incarnate One. I do not attempt to retrace any of these steps in the present chapter. Only let me again claim for that last aspect of the doctrine of the Spirit the most earnest, reverent, loving attention of the believer, as he 'lives by faith in the Son of God' (Gal. 2:20). A great wealth of spiritual blessing surely lies ready for use, for the Christian who will recollect it and use it, in the truth of the Spirit's work for, on and in, the incarnate Lord. That work, that unspeakably deep and precious connection of the Spirit with the Redeemer in the work and redemption, is meant to throw the full light of life eternal upon *our* connection by the Spirit with Christ Jesus, who is our life. We shall recur often to this side of truth in later pages; but let it be kept always in view. We, everyone of us who believe on the name of the Son of God, are 'joined unto him, one Spirit' (1 Cor. 6:17). Our contact, our union, our embodiment, is such as to be rightly described in the holy Word by that surprising phrase.

And is not light thrown upon the phrase by the

remembrance that the Spirit who has given us our life, who has imparted to us Christ, is indeed the Spirit of Christ, not only in the inner relations of Deity, but in the blessed incarnation of our glorious Head? He who is himself thus doubly united to Christ – if I may express it so – can he not indeed with the richest and holiest fulness pour into us, Christ's members, the power and virtues of our Head? Indeed he can. And we, therefore, the favoured members, will bear that fact in wondering and loving memory. We will cherish it in our heart of hearts. We will use it in our hourly life. Having the Spirit, we will remember how fully and truly by the Spirit we possess the Son. And in weakness, in sadness, in temptation, under the burdening sense it may be of spiritual decline, we will without delay or misgiving *use* our wonderful treasure. We will by the Spirit *enjoy* our possession of the Son, not after the hour of need, but in it. With such a bond to such a Head, why should we for one minute walk in failure? Nay, 'when we are weak, then we are strong'; 'in the name of the Lord Jesus, and by the Spirit of our God' (2 Cor. 12:10; 1 Cor. 6:11).

And now to advance more directly to the study of the work of the Holy Spirit 'for us men and our salvation'. And do thou, most blessed Spirit of God, shine on us and in us as we go!

It might seem right that we should here first consider his divine work in creation, in the 'old creation', in 'nature'. For in a large range of Scripture passages, from Genesis 1:2 onwards, we find him mysteriously but distinctly revealed as the immediate divine Agent in the making and manipulation, so to speak, of material things.

But our proposed subject is the Spirit's work *in*

redemption, a subject which will indeed give us material enough. All I would do here is to call attention in a general way to this Scriptural connection of the *Spirit* with the world of Matter. It is one among the many suggestions in the divine Word that matter has for its immediate basis the absolutely immaterial will and power of God. And, like all those other suggestions, it reminds the believer, as he rests on his God for *spiritual* life and power, that the whole *material* universe, wrought by the same will that saves him, is infinitely pliable in its Maker's hands for the ultimate good of his spiritual new creation.

Reverently leaving alone, then, this field of truth, I turn deliberately to another for some brief but earnest recollections and suggestions. That other field is the *work of the Holy Spirit in relation to the Holy Scriptures.*

I hardly need say that I am aware of the present gravity of that subject, and of the extreme difficulty of speaking upon it to edification amidst the unsettlement, and indeed tumult, of present speculations and negations. But it may be both possible and helpful to take it up in this chapter along a line single, in a sense simple, and yet all-important. We will adhere strictly to the terms of our great subject – the Holy Spirit's work in relation to the Scriptures.

It appears to me that many widely prevalent, present views of the nature and function of the written Word, however much truth of detail may enter into their formation, err in their *ensemble* by their deeply human-itarian, naturalistic character. Taking up the perfectly true position that human agency and natural process are largely present as factors in the production of Scripture, many an able theorist declines, or however fails, to see that nevertheless the resultant of the factors of production is not humanitarian, nor naturalistic, but the divine Word, the supernatural Oracle.

All this failure is the effect far less of a patient and inductive study of the phenomena than of the general influence of the modern tendency to simplify and unify phenomena under laws as general as possible. It comes not a little of an instinctive wish to see a likeness, a homogeneity, and ultimately a one-ness, under all spiritual operations and experiences.

And so the 'inspiration' of prophet and apostle is classified as the same in *genus,* and even in *species,* as the 'inspiration' of the Christian believer of our day in his walk of faith and obedience; as a development – in some respects very high, no doubt, but still only a development – of the general 'consciousness' of the church and its members. Isaiah, or the Isaiahs, and Paul, were inspired undoubtedly; but so, and in essentially the same way, were Augustine and Anselm, Tauler and Savonarola, Luther and Bunyan, Oberlin and Elizabeth Fry, nay Plato and Virgil, Shakespeare and Wordsworth, nay the earnest explorer of the structure and processes of material nature, or of the human spirit, or of the written products of that spirit, in whatever region, 'secular' or 'sacred', human or divine. To all Christian minds and lives, indeed to all grave and elevated minds and lives, Christian or not, some fragments of eternal verities have been somehow disclosed. These they have rendered into word, or act, or both, not always exactly, not always truly, perhaps not always even truthfully, but still so as to give some hints and 'broken lights' of the eternal archetype and original. To the devout men who produced the biblical literature such disclosures were made in a very remarkable degree, and Scripture accordingly gives us hints of archetypal and eternal truths, in a very remarkable way. But to them, as to others, those hints were conveyed only *naturally,* through their moral nature, through experience and reflection. And so in order to gather up these hints given in the Bible we have to

> 'look
> Wisely upon it, as another book.'[1]

We have to get the gold of eternal truth out of the rock of an indefinite amount of human prejudice, mistake, and partial points of view on the part of the human reporters of the truth. We are to expect more gold, no doubt, from quarrying the Psalms, and the Gospels, and the Epistles than from quarrying the *Phœdo,* or the *Divina Commedia,* or the *Pilgrim's Progress.* But we dig our shaft and sift our diggings in precisely the same way in all the cases.

I am very well aware with what mental energy and skill, along with what a range and depth of various knowledge, such theories in many instances have been constructed and propagated – I hardly need say now 'defended', so vast a currency have they obtained. Comparatively few and far

---

1.   '"And now,' he cried, 'I shall be pleased to get
        'Beyond the Bible – there I puzzle yet.'

        '"he spoke abash'd – 'Nay, nay!' the friend replied,
        'You need not lay the good old book aside;
        'Antique and curious, I myself indeed
        Read it at times, but as a man should read;
        'A fine old work it is, and I protest
        'I hate to hear it treated as a jest;
        'The book of wisdom in it, if you look
        'Wisely upon it, as another book.'"
                        Crabbe, *Zale 21, The Learned Boy.*

between are the modern literary theologians who quite
definitely and unmistakably hold that the Holy Scriptures
are truly and properly *sui generis* among books as being
(as well as containing) the Word of God, and as carrying
in a way quite of their own that precious thing, *Divine
Authority*. But I also recollect that in many a past period
and crisis the deep tide of intellectual consciousness has
taken directions which, on the whole, needed afterwards
to be reversed, on a fuller discovery or more calm and
reverent review of great facts which had remained all the
while unaltered. And I humbly believe that the day will
come when the intellectual consciousness of biblical
scientific students as a class will be vastly more alive than
it is now to the superhuman and authoritative aspect of
the Holy Bible and to the immense significance of that
aspect. And such a change of general mental attitude will
vastly modify many present theories about the construction
of the Bible, theories built much less than is sometimes
thought upon the whole facts.

What I attempt to do here is simply to recall my reader's
attention earnestly, gravely, and with deep conviction to
the witness which the Holy Scripture bears to its own
unique character among books of the Book whose author
is none other than the third person of the blessed Trinity.
And need I say that this is no argument in a circle? I ask
the Bible to witness to the Bible; but I ask the Bible as
literature, as history, to witness to the Bible as revelation,
oracular, authoritative, divine. As history, capable of
verification, it shows to me Jesus Christ, God and man,
living, dying, rising, proving himself to be profoundly,
ultimately trustworthy. But this Jesus Christ, as presented
in the same historical mirror, is seen laying one hand upon

the prophets and the other upon the apostles, and bidding his followers regard with an altogether unique attention their uttered messages. And I attend accordingly to those messages. And in them I find disclosures and intimations as to the quality and authority of the biblical writings as the oracles of God, which, if words have meaning, put those writings – as to their total character – on a level different in kind from all other literature. I find nothing to forbid me to ask, with deep reverence, whether human personality and natural process were not factors to the product; and I assuredly find that they were. But I find it emphasized with vastly greater earnestness and fulness that so did the other factor of ultimate divine authorship govern and manipulate the lower factor that the true designer and architect of the Book has *had his way* all along, in the total and in the details too.

I find nothing to enable me to define, in any full or exhaustive way most certainly, the *mode* of the supreme author's management of the subordinate authors. I find nothing to tell me 'what it felt like to be inspired'. In many and many a case, I can well believe it 'felt like' – nothing; nothing distinguishable from other things. I can well believe that when Paul wrote to Philemon he 'felt' nothing supernatural, any more than when Luther wrote to Melanchthon, or Newton to Cowper. *I do not say that it was so;* but it may have been so, for all that we are told. On the other hand I not only can believe, but am sure, that Daniel and John received their revelations in a state manifestly and entirely abnormal, as Abraham and Moses on certain occasions had done before them; unless we are to put quietly aside the profoundly solemn assertions to this effect made in Scripture as if they were so much poetical and imaginative excrescence, or framework, because there is so little in human experience outside the Scripture, outside this record of the divine redemption of fallen man, to verify them. Yes, it is impossible to define or describe scriptural inspiration as a subjective experience. The *mode,* as to any general account of it, is unknown. 'Our theory is not to have a theory.' But I do find abundant testimony on the historic surface of the New Testament Scriptures for the strong and unalterable conviction, sure as the historical reality of Jesus Christ our Lord, that a humanitarian, naturalistic view of Scripture is wholly and gravely inadequate to meet the mysterious facts.

I find our Lord and Master himself handling the Old Testament Scriptures with the manner of one who not only owns their general significance but personally cherishes, I dare to say reveres, their *authority,* even in details of expression; and I find him doing this not only in the early stages of his course but even more in the latter, in the last. And I see him doing it nowhere more fully and unreservedly than when he has overcome death (Luke 24), and come back from the unseen in the power of endless life. And when, exalted into heaven, he 'sends' the blessed Paraclete, his own promised representative, the Spirit of Truth, I find that one main result of the glorious emission was the incessant use by the apostles of the writings of the prophets, in precisely the spirit, no less and no more, of their Master before them.

And I observe one remarkable phenomenon of the whole case. I find that the Lord and the apostles make comparatively little, if I may reverently say so, of the sacred *writers* of the Old Testament and comparatively everything of the sacred *writings.* They dwell not so much on *who said it* as on *what is written.* No grades of authority appear in their estimate. What stands within the scrolls of what we familiarly call the Old Testament, and what he called the Law, the Prophets, and the Psalms, is in the eyes of Jesus Christ his Father's Word, whatever else it is. As such it is his weapon in the Temptation, his credential on the Mount of the Sermon, his mysterious solace in the Garden, his death-word on the Cross, his theme upon the Emmaus Road on the Easter afternoon, and in the Upper Chamber where he stood that evening in his immortality. Oh blessed road and blessed chamber! Let us often take our Bibles out with us on the one, up with us to the other. We shall be the less likely then to think that to 'look on the Bible as on another book' is to look upon it 'wisely', even from the point of view of the strictest induction of truth from facts.

But now all this mysterious Divinity of the Bible, this properly miraculous character of it, this nature of it so entirely refusing to be accounted for by natural process and human consciousness, is assigned by itself not to God in general only, but to the *Holy Spirit* in particular. This is our immediate concern in this enquiry. The statement of the fact is almost all the treatment I give to it; but what a fact it is to state!

He who as the divine agent in the blessed incarnation, he who made and sustained the manhood of the second Adam, adjusting it with infinite skill to the blessed filial Godhead, it is he who is the divine agent in this glorious parallel process, the construction of Scripture. He, the all-blessed Spirit, in that double union of his with Christ of which we spoke above, so managed the long antecedent march of prophecy, both its substance and its phraseology, that Moses, whatever was the prophet's 'consciousness' in writing (John 5:46, 47), wrote of Christ; and 'David in the Spirit' (Matt. 22:43) called him his Master; and Isaiah (John 12:39-41) saw his glory and spake of him; yes, so that the risen Redeemer himself found '*in all the Scriptures* the things concerning himself' (Luke 24:27). So did he design, mani-pulate, and accomplish that 'every Scripture hath in it the Spirit of God'[1] (2 Tim. 3:16). So did he fashion 'the Word' that it is 'the sword of the Spirit' (Eph. 6:17). So did he speak by the prophets that when an apostolic writer quotes the words of Jeremiah (Heb. 10:15-17) he ignores, as it were, the prophet's personality, intense, tender, and profoundly interesting, and instructive as that particular personality was. *Majoribus intentus est;* he is aiming deeper. He is citing the words as capable of carrying authoritative, decisive weight on eternal principles and facts. And he sees nothing for that purpose but their *ultimate* authorship: 'Whereof *the Holy Ghost* also is a witness unto us; for after that he had said before, This is the covenant that I will make with them after those days, saith the Lord; I will put my laws into their hearts, and in their minds will I write them, [then said he,] And their sins and their iniquities will I remember no more' (Jer. 31:33, 34). The words are, in a sense, in a true sense, Jeremiah's. But for the writer to the Hebrews they are simply the words of the Holy Ghost. And so they must be to us, let me add, if we would lean the whole weight of our human need on them in life and in the hour of death. Evacuate Scripture of its divine authority, and you so far paralyse its power for divine consolation.

---

1. The rendering, 'Every Scripture inspired of God *is also profitable,*' is not demanded by the Greek. Compare the Greek of 1 Timothy 4:4.

I thus state something of the outline of the revealed facts of this great and inestimably precious work of the Holy Spirit. I well know that it is but a fragment; it is but a suggestion; it is, in some of its parts, little more than a confession of faith, and a confession of a kind not always very easy to make at the present time. But such as it is, I make it to my reader as in the presence of our Lord and Master. At this period in the history of the church, if I mistake not, it is important in the highest degree to hold fast, and to hold in the foreground of our convictions and our consciousness, the supernatural, the miraculous, the divinely authoritative, aspect of the Holy Scriptures, as the work throughout of none other than the Holy Spirit of God, the blessed Lord of truth and light.

That conviction leaves me, as I have said, free to enquire into the mode and the materials of the construction of the scriptural books by their human sub-authors; but with one important exception. It does not leave me free, as I believe, to entertain the theory that any book of the holy canon, being as to its ultimate authorship the work of the Spirit of Truth, was from the side of its human authorship, a late fabrication, whose writer sought to borrow an illegitimate prestige by the use of a venerated name and an immemorial date, other than his own.

In conclusion, if indeed the holy Book is thus the work and word of the Holy Spirit, we have good cause to turn with humble and glad expectation to that Spirit, who dwells in Christ and in us, to open up to the inmost soul as we read it the things of Christ which, according to Christ, are in it everywhere.

Let me quote a few sentences from that grand and 'Fruitful Exhortation to the Reading and Knowledge of the Holy Scripture', our First Homily of the First Book, and to conclude:

'The Scripture is full as well of low valleys, plain ways, and easy for every man to use and to walk in, as also of high hills and mountains, which few men can climb unto. And "whosoever giveth his mind to Holy Scripture with diligent study and burning desire, it cannot be," saith John Chrysostom, "that he should be left without help. For either God Almighty will send him some godly doctor to teach him, ... or else, if we lack a learned man to instruct and teach us, yet God himself from above, will give light unto our minds, and teach us those things which are necessary for us, and wherein we be ignorant." And in another place Chrysostom saith that "man's human and worldly wisdom needeth not to the understanding of Scripture, but the revelation of the Holy Ghost, who inspireth the true meaning unto them that with humility and diligence do search therefor."'

'Here is the cause of all our evils,' says the same Chrysostom,[2] 'our not knowing the Scriptures.'

---

2. *Τουτο παντων αίτιον των κακων, το μη είδεναι τας γραφας.* This is but a specimen of the language about Scripture used by the Fathers of the first centuries. And yet their age was an age of seething speculation and discussion. They would scarcely have endorsed what has been recently said (not by a Romanist), 'The Bible is the most dangerous of God's gifts to man.'

Chapter 4

The Holy Spirit and Regeneration

The previous three chapters are in some measure introductory only. Let us proceed now to the more detailed study of our sacred subject, by the method, at once the simplest and the surest, of taking up some of the great passages of scriptural revelation and discourse upon it and listening anew to their message in reverent, believing meditation. And as we do so we will remember that the blessed Spirit is not only the true author of the written Word, but also its supreme and true expositor. Not all my readers know the noble hymn, found in few modern collections, strange to say, in which Cowper has set this forth; And I quote it accordingly in full:

'The Spirit breathes upon the word,
    And brings the truth to sight:
Precepts and promises afford
    A sanctifying light.

'A glory gilds the sacred page
    Majestic, like the sun;
It gives a light to every age;
    It gives, but borrows none.

'The hand that gave it still supplies
    The gracious light and heat;
his truths upon the nations rise;
    They rise, but never set.

'Let everlasting thanks be thine,
    For such a bright display
As makes the world of darkness shine
    With beams of heavenly day.

'My soul rejoices to pursue
    The steps of him I love,
Till glory breaks upon my view
    In brighter worlds above.'

It is true; we need the author to be also, in the inmost
secret of the matter, the expositor, the interpreter. Then
will the written Word shine, like the living Word, with
the light as of a transfiguration, its countenance and its
garments also. Then shall we trace all through the holy
pages 'the steps of him we love', of him who has himself
assured us that they are to be found there (Luke 24:25, 27,
44, 45; John 5:39).

It may be well here, however, to say one word of caution
as to the use made by the Christian of this truth of the
Spirit's expository work. *How* may we expect him
normally to exercise for us this merciful function? Is it by
direct illumination, such that this text or that passage shall
be seen by the soul, in the way of supernatural intuition,
to mean this or that? If I am not mistaken, this impression
is widely spread among Christians; and I would not lightly
or without sympathy speak in correction of it. Nevertheless
it must be obvious, on reflection, that to expect the Holy
One to act upon us in such a manner as this is to expect
the gift, just so far as such action goes, of prophetic
infallibility. It makes my interpretation, arrived at under
such illumination, as truly a divine revelation as the text

itself, and it precludes any criticism of my interpretation, because it thus is, at least in essentials, the interpretation of God. When I hear or read, as I sometimes do, that a Christian believer speaks of this or that as having been 'shown to him' in such and such a text, I am well aware that the meaning of the phrase, as the speaker intends it, *may* be most true, healthful, and trustworthy. But it is also possible that it may involve a claim, a dangerous claim, to hold and teach the interpretation in question as one above examination, because inspired, because divinely intuitive.

What then are we to think of the matter? Are we, after all, to apply ourselves to Scripture study without special prayer and special expectation? Are we to assume practically that 'the natural man *doth* receive the things of the Spirit of God' (See 1 Cor. 2:14); that they are *not* 'foolishness unto him'; that they are not, necessarily and only, 'spiritually discerned'? Shall we, after all, in face of all that we recollected in the previous chapter, think that to look on the Bible as on 'another book' is to look upon it 'wisely'? No; the mistake of doing so is not only great but fatal in our Scripture study, and we will not make it. We clergy at least, in the words of our Second Ordination Service, 'will continually pray to God the Father, through the mediation of our only Saviour Jesus Christ, for the heavenly assistance of the Holy Ghost, that by daily reading and weighing of the Scriptures we may wax riper and stronger in our ministry.' And what the clergyman thus does in view of his special function, the private Christian will do in view of his; in view of his sacred 'ministry', his 'work of ministry' (Eph. 4:12), his whole life as laid at the Lord's feet for his use.

But the point is this. We shall ask, not for mental

infallibility, which is asking in effect for a gift that has been 'annulled' (1 Cor. 13:8), but for spiritual submission, receptivity, and harmony with the Spirit of God, such that our reverent inquiry into the meaning of the Spirit's words may be carried on in spiritually 'dry light' (1 Cor. 2:13). We shall pray for such presence and power of the Holy One within us, at the 'springs of thought and will', that we may be *morally* ready for the least hint, the tenderest suggestion, given in the blessed Book, about the will and mind of the author of the Book. Such a prayer will on the one hand recognize at every step our helplessness where we really are helpless. It will on the other hand only quicken us in the diligent and patient work of attention, and research, and comparison, as we use that precious mental faculty, which the Lord who made us, and remade us, has given us to be used in his presence and for him. And the result will be no mere prolonged uncertainty, as if we were perpetually in fear lest new scriptural evidence should upset our deepest spiritual certainties. By the grace of God it will be a calm and settled certainty, solid yet developing, and the resultant of spiritual simplicity and of the genuine mental discovery and acquisition which such simplicity powerfully assists. It will be a certainty, as to all things of salvation, practically absolute to ourselves. But it will be kept clear of all untenable claims to have *prophetic authority over others.*

I have digressed at some length. And I would close my digression with an appeal, all the more earnest after the cautions on which I have ventured, to make the closing verses of 1 Corinthians 2, after all, one of our ruling mottoes for all study of the Word of God.

Approaching now some of the great Scriptural passages which discourse of the Holy Spirit and his work, I observe that these are to be found, in the main, in the writings of John and of Paul. I propose then to take some such passages from each of these apostles in turn, and to examine their witness, with a special view always to the spiritual life of myself and of my reader. Paul's writings will afford us several such passages, mainly from the Roman, Corinthian, Galatian, and Ephesian epistles. In John's Gospel we have, above all things, the precious Discourse of the Upper Chamber (John 14–16), but also passages in the third, seventh and twentieth chapters. In the first epistle we have much incidental material. In the Revelation the blessed Spirit appears again and again, and in connections full of doctrinal and spiritual teaching.

Let us take John's Gospel first, both because it comes first in the canon, and because in it, with scarcely any exception, the teaching about the Spirit comes from the very lips of the Son. The passage of passages here is the Paschal Discourse. But some shorter, while all-important, passages precede it, which we now take up, for brief but most reverent meditation on their divine instruction.

The first passage, the only one I can touch at present, is the first part of the conversation with Nicodemus (John 3:1-8).

How shall I deal with it? First, necessarily, by excluding from the inquiry many extremely interesting subsidiary points. I do not forget, but I must not now consider, the connecting 'but', or 'now', (unaccountably omitted by the Authorized Version), which links the passage to the statements just before. I do not forget, but I must now pass by, the question what precise motive brought

Nicodemus to the Lord, and what led the Lord to speak instantly to him about the *kingdom* and entrance into it. And indeed I do not forget the weighty importance of the passage in the study of the doctrine of Christian baptism, to which I cannot doubt reference is made in the word 'water' (John 3:5), though I know that much has been thoughtfully said on the other side. But I do not dwell upon this now. Not that I undervalue the momentousness of the question raised; not that I regard the divine sacrament with feelings other than humble reverence and thankfulness. But I believe that the passage contains elements of truth which have usually received far less attention, certainly in current thought in the church at large, than the baptismal reference has received, and which yet have the most important bearing on that reference, such that they should help to interpret it rather than it claim to explain them. And these elements I find above all in verse 8: 'The wind bloweth where it listeth, and thou hearest the sound thereof, but canst not tell whence it cometh, and whither it goeth; so is every one that is born of the Spirit.' 'Ye must be born again.'

Take this sacred utterance up in detail.

1. '*Born* of the Spirit.' Read the phrase as if new, as if in a recently discovered document of the first century. How powerful the term is, how profound! The word is not merely altered, influenced, reformed, reinvigorated. It is born, born again, born from above, touched with a *biogenesis* which is indeed the impartation of a higher order of life, for it is life eternal. The man is taken back to a new beginning, set going again under new provisions and conditions of life, stamped with a new spiritual

impression, the living family likeness of the sons of God. Would we estimate the weight and fulness of what is meant by this wonderful phrase? Then let us take the New Testament, and examine again, under the Spirit's illumination on our spirits (e.g. Rom. 8; 1 John 3; 5) all the many passages where 'childhood' and 'sonship' of the spiritual kind are spoken of; the places which direct us how to know the 'children of God', what are their notes and marks, what are their characteristic thoughts of God, of Christ, of the brethren of Christ, what, in short, they *are*, and what they *do*, as 'the sons and daughters of the Lord Almighty' (2 Cor. 6:18). 'Whosoever is born of God overcometh the world'; 'As many as are led by the Spirit of God, they are the sons of God'; 'Behold, what manner of love, that we should be called the sons of God. Therefore the world knoweth us not, because it knew him not.' These are celestial words, penetrating and searching the soul. Well may Augustine say, 'Let all sign themselves with the Cross, let all say the Amen and the Hallelujah, let all be baptized, let all enter the church doors; the children of God are distinguished from the children of the devil only by love. They who have love are born of God; they who have not love are not.'

2. 'Born of *the Spirit*.' To him, the blessed third person, the sacred Subject of our studies, the Lord Jesus Christ here assigns the immediate agency in the new birth. HE takes in hand the man, and deals with him in regenerating efficacy. He conveys to him the eternal life whose secret and at the same time whose manifestation is love generated of the love of God. He ploughs the ground of the soul, convincing it of sin, righteousness, and judgment. He

52   THE HOLY SPIRIT

inserts the vivifying seed, so that the man is 'born again
by the word of God, which liveth and abideth for ever' (1
Pet. 1:23). He 'pours out the love of God in the heart'
(Rom. 5:5). He both gives the child-state and teaches the
new-born man to understand it, to cry 'Abba Father' (Rom.
8:15; Gal. 4:6), 'the Abba, that prayer of faith alone', to
the eternal and Invisible.

3. 'So is everyone that is born of the Spirit.' We come last
to the first word of this divine sentence: 'So.' Of the 'men',
of the human beings, thus born again, born of the Spirit, a
certain something is universally, is at the very least,
normally true; true not of some of them, not of a kind or
class among them, but of 'every one'.

The reference of 'so' is clear, is unmistakable. The Lord
has just used a familiar but vivid illustration as was his
wont. He has spoken of the breath of air, the 'spirit' of
material nature, of its mystery and of its evidence. In certain
of its phenomena he sees the counterpart of the case of
'every one that is born of the Spirit'.

And this in three main respects, which I briefly indicate,
though perhaps there is slight need that I should do so.

First, there is in the two cases an analogous *secrecy of
process.* The breathing atmosphere fans my forehead, plays
in the tree above me, whispers in the grass and rushes of
the riverside below me. It is in itself meanwhile an
infinitely delicate and quite invisible wave or current in
the airy ocean; and all the combined observation and
inference of mankind could not tell – certainly I could not
tell – where that wave in the pure deep began and where it
will sink into repose again. '*So* is every one that is born of
the Spirit'; the process is mysterious. The man receives a

divine power upon him, within him. He is alive unto God, knowing him, loving him, lovingly bent upon pleasing him 'as his own son that serveth him' (Mal. 3:17). And he knows that he did not originate for himself this condition; he did not beget and bear himself again to living hope, to loving life. Perhaps he knows definitely when, in some day or hour of mercy, he was awakened, convinced, enlightened, enabled to give himself to God. But this is but part of the secret, one mighty symptom of the process. He does not know when and how the holy work really began, how long the Spirit, who brought him to the new birth at last, who was, in Hooker's words, 'thus effectual in the secret work of regeneration unto newness of life', had been preparing for that bright hour, by secret pleadings, by unnoticed providences, by even slighted means of grace – slighted, yet leaving *some* mark on thought and will. He may know when the wind manifestly swayed him; he does not know from whence and how it came on its holy path. And truly he knows not whither it goeth; 'it doth not yet appear what he shall be' (1 John 3:2).

Secondly, the air-wave illustrates the mystery of the new birth by its *independence as regards the will of man.* Putting aside exceptions which are altogether trivial, the streams of the vast atmospheric ocean do indeed not obey the will of man. He cannot originate, he cannot steer for one mile, for one yard, the broad current either of the zephyr of the summer evening or of 'the storms that wrecks the winter sky'. From his point of view 'it bloweth where it listeth'. Even so the Spirit 'distributeth', divideth, giveth, moveth 'as he will' (1 Cor. 12:1). The sons of God are 'born, not of the will of the flesh, nor of the will of man, but of God' (John 1:13). It is a truth never meant to discourage, to repel, to bewilder; for this sovereignty of will is the sovereignty of him whose 'fruit is love, joy, peace' (Gal. 5:22), of him concerning whom it is written, 'Your heavenly Father shall give his Holy Spirit to them that ask him' (Luke 11:13). But it is a truth meant to humble, meant to keep us low indeed before the eternal Will.

Thirdly, the new birth is illustrated by the action of the wind in respect of *evidence given in results*. Here is one plain point in our blessed Lord's parable, all-important, yet often overlooked. The wave of air, in its origin, course and issues, is mysterious, invisible, undefinable; but its presence around me and in my surroundings is to be known by practical results, and by them alone; 'Thou hearest the sound, the voice.' The trees of the wood, the waters of the mountain lake, you 'hear the wind' in them and on them; and thus you ascertain its presence there. 'So is every one that is born of the Spirit'; every one. The divinely mysterious process produces known and observable effects; and its presence, its presence not in the abstract but here or there, is to be verified by them, and by them alone. Regeneration, the coming to be one of the children of God, in Augustine's sense of that term, in John the apostle's sense, in the Lord's sense, is indeed a 'secret thing' in itself; but its evidences are practical and plain. The Spirit is eternal, divine; but where he effectually works the new birth, there, in one degree or another, so says the Lord here, you will hear the sound, you will trace results. And what *is* the sound of the heavenly Wind in the being, the life? It consists of things which indeed belong to, though they are not the creatures of, the circumstances of the common day: 'love, joy, peace, longsuffering, gentleness, goodness, faithfulness, meekness, self-control' (Gal. 5:22, 23). It consists, in fact, of love, love in distribution, heaven-given love to God and to man in God.

It will be obvious that these remarks have much to do, supposing them to be true, with our interpretation of the function of the blessed sacrament of baptism, and in particular of the language of our own baptismal ritual. Into the deeply interesting and important questions so suggested, questions scriptural, ecclesiastical, historical, questions amongst others of the nature of the absolute language of ceremony as against the more guarded language of biography, I do not enter here, for I think they are not in place in these meditations. Only it is right that I should say for my own part that not one word above written has been written in forgetfulness of my obligations as a presbyter of the English Church, or with faltering convictions as to the rightness of the language of its sacramental ritual. All the more earnestly would I say, and not least to my brethren in the ministry of the Word and sacraments. Let nothing, absolutely nothing, be allowed to obscure our sense of the unutterable moral weight of our Redeemer's words in this great passage of John: 'Ye must be born again. So is every one that is born of the Spirit.'

William Beveridge, Bishop of St. Asaph (1704–1708), was no half-hearted Churchman. Among our elder divines few use language about the holy Sacraments more reverent, I might say more rapturous, than his. Let me close then with a brief extract from his seventy-third printed sermon, *Christ's Resurrection the Cause of our Regeneration*:

'By your care and pains about the things of this world you may perhaps get something in it, and perhaps not, and how much so ever it be, it is nothing at all in comparison of what the children of God all have; "all things are theirs", all things that God hath made, and he himself too that made them. And what can they desire more? There is nothing more for them to desire; and therefore their minds must needs be at rest, and their souls as full as they can hold of all true joy and comfort.

'Who then would not be in the number of these blessed souls? Who would not be regenerate, and made a child of God, if he might? And who may not, if he will? Blessed be God, we are all as yet capable of it, for now that Christ is risen from the dead and exalted at the right hand of God, to be a Prince and a Saviour, to give repentance and forgiveness of sins, if we do but apply ourselves to him and believe and trust on him for it, his Father will be ours too; he will beget us again in his own likeness, and admit us into the glorious liberty of his own children.'

Chapter 5

The Holy Spirit and Conviction of Sin

Our last thoughts were given to the work of the Holy Spirit as he effects the new birth. We considered him as he deals with man 'dead in trespasses and sins' (Eph. 2:1), and brings him into that wonderful 'newness of life' in which 'henceforth' he is to 'walk by the Spirit', possessing 'the Spirit of adoption in whom we cry Abba, Father' (Rom. 6:4; Gal. 5:25; Rom. 8:15).

'Our quicken'd souls awake and rise
From the long sleep of death;
On heavenly things we fix our eyes,
And praise employs our breath.'

In the present chapter I ask my reader to take a step in some sense backward. In studying the work of regeneration we also studied, by reason of the spiritual connection of the two things, some of the phenomena of conversion; that wonderful turning about of the inward man which corresponds as nearly as possible in its idea to the great Scripture word, repentance. For let it never be forgotten that repentance means more, very much more, than regret, or even remorse, or even 'godly sorrow'. It is a deep, decisive alteration in the attitude of the soul towards God, and his glory and his claim, and his salvation. 'The sinner that repenteth' (Luke 15:7-10) is the sinner that is converted, turned back, brought back from loss to

57

salvation, from the wilderness to the fold, from the far-off land to the Father's home.

This however is by the way. I was recalling the fact that we have already considered some of the main phenomena of that blessed change which is as to its divine secret and agency new birth, and as to its human experience conversion. And thus we take in some sort a step backward to consider now the great initial step of that work as wrought by the Spirit, whether for the world or the soul, that step which is called *conviction of sin*. This line of inquiry, however, will not be retrograde in any unreasonable way. Not seldom a great subject is best studied first by a brief view of its whole, and then by closer attention to its parts. In this chapter and in some subsequent pages we will deal thus with the decisive work of our blessed life-giver, looking for his merciful light.

The Scripture which puts prominently forward the convincing work of the Holy Spirit is, I hardly need to say, John 16:8-11; part of that divine discourse to which we owe, as we have remembered already, our central revelations about the blessed Spirit's personality, and about very much of his work. The wording of this particular passage calls of course for most careful study. And so I would not fail to notice two leading features of it; first, that it speaks of the Spirit's convincing work as done in and on 'the world', distinguished from the disciples of Jesus; secondly, that it connects that work in the closest way with the Lord Jesus Christ himself: 'because they believe not on me'; 'because I go to my Father'. Nor do I forget that 'conviction of *sin*' is only one of three convictions spoken of in the passage; I do not lose sight of the 'righteousness' and the 'judgment'. But on this latter point it will appear, I think, as we go on that so close is the relation of the two latter convictions to the first, and that they are in some respects so subordinated to the first, that we may venture lawfully to group the whole work under the title of 'conviction of sin'.

Now first a few words on the reference of this great work 'to the world', that is to the mass of unregenerate humanity. It has been thought by some interpreters that this mention of the world excludes from the passage a distinct reference to the Spirit's saving operation in individual souls. And so the point and bearing of the Saviour's sentences here has been supposed to be directed towards what I may call *public human opinion* about Christ's character and work, and about the momentous awfulness of *sin,* as the great contradiction to *righteousness* (now glorified in Christ), and as the sure subject of coming *judgment* to be exercised by Christ, who has already given earnest of his final exercise of judgeship in his victory over the world's prince. In this view, we are to look for the fulfilment and explanation of the words in such great phenomena as, for instance, the awe which fell upon the Jews as a nation when the Pentecostal effusion came and the gospel work began; an awe indicated in one way or another all through the Acts.

Or again, to take a yet larger example, we may look for the fulfilment in that greatly deepened sense (for such it is) in the shame of wrong, and the glory of righteousness, and the depth and solemnity of coming retribution, which has pervaded mankind as a mass wherever Christianity has been, even inadequately, proclaimed. And certainly this is one of the greatest facts of human history, however it is explained. And to the believer, no explanation of it will be adequate which does not connect it with the work of the Holy Spirit upon the human conscience, as he makes the human soul able to interpret to itself, however dimly, the moral and spiritual significance of the person, character and sacrifice of Jesus Christ. And it is perfectly true that such public, general, universal conviction may, and alas continually does, fall quite short in individuals of the conviction which 'worketh repentance unto salvation'; and that therefore it may be studied as a work which moves outside the inner circles of the Spirit's saving action upon souls; as a work emphatically in *the world*.

But all this says only, at most, that the words of our Master in John 16 do, or may, refer to a so to speak indefinite and diffused operation of the Spirit, but it does not say that they do not also, and in a special and central degree, refer to his inner circles of effectual blessing. For surely wherever that effectual blessing takes place, wherever a soul in its mysterious individual personality is awakened from the sleep of sin and born of the Spirit, it is a case in which a member of 'the world' has been dealt with, in the world, to be brought out of the world. It is a case in which the blessed agent, like him whom he glorifies, has gone into the outer wilderness, and has led from it a rescued wanderer, lately dead in sins, blinded by the god of this world, 'walking according to its course' (Eph. 2:2). In this new convert, whether from open heathenism or heresy or infidelity, or from a profession of the blessed faith which is in name only, we find just the general facts of 'the world' individualized. Just that which, in a sense less definite and intense, is done by the Spirit for the world as world, is done by the same Spirit in a sense most definite, most effectual, for this member of the world as individual will and soul. He has brought the man to 'conviction of sin, righteousness, and judgement', in the light of Christ.

And it is manifest, by the way, that the large, wide, work of conviction in the sphere of general opinion is done in no small measure through these isolated occurrences, these deep individual convictions of sin. So it has been from the beginning. The thousands of definite convictions, repentances and baptisms at Pentecost were a mighty means for diffusing through the Jewish public mind an impression about Christ and the gospel far short indeed in itself of regeneration and salvation, yet incalculably precious and important. And so it is to this day. Nothing can more powerfully contribute to keep up, and to raise up, 'the world's' public consciousness of sin, righteousness and judgment than the presence in it, as salt-grains in the mass, of individuals intensely and savingly convinced of these three things for themselves, in the light of immediate dealings for themselves with God in Christ. And nothing would so fatally lower 'the world's' public moral and quasi-Christian consciousness as that such individual convictions, such personally convinced ones, should become few and fewer, till religion itself should be dissociated in common opinion from the very ideas conveyed by the words, '*I* have sinned against the Lord'; 'What must *I* do to be saved?'

So without misgiving I take these words of the Lord Jesus, and see in them his assurance that the Holy Spirit, in the gospel age, and as the divine messenger to souls, and illuminator of souls about himself the Saviour, should convince the individual unregenerate heart, in merciful speciality, of sin, and righteousness, and judgment. He should 'open' it to 'attend to' its unspeakable *need* of Christ (Acts 16:14); and the *sin* against the love of God, and against itself, of indifference or refusal in presence of a manifested Christ; and to the lawful glory of *righteousness,* the eternal antithesis to the transgression of the law, a glory now transcendently displayed in the exaltation of the crucified Christ Jesus to the heavens; and to the ineffable rightness, certainty and eternity of the *judicial ruin* of sin and all that sides with sin – a ruin already in effect accomplished by the personal triumph of the Son of God over his mysterious personal antagonist, the world's prince and god. So, according to this passage, should the Spirit of truth, holiness and love deal with the individual. Such should be the personal conviction of sin, righteousness and judgment under his operating hand. In a way that should make use of all the moral faculties of the man, and yet should work from infinitely above them, and penetrate if it be possible beneath them, he should bring the inner eyes to see something of the realities of this great matter, so that the man should say with the voice of his inmost being, 'I have sinned against the Lord and his glorious Christ; what must I do?'

May I make bold to turn to my reader, and laying aside the tone of mere enquiry and discussion, speak to him, as to a brother man? I venture to ask you, does this brief, fragmentary indication of the Spirit's sin-convincing work correspond in any degree to your consciousness, your experience? Ah, surely it does. For indeed such things have been taking place in souls ever since the day when at the great effusion, *and as its very first result,* three thousand human individuals 'were pricked in their heart, and said, Men and brethren, what shall we do?' (Acts 2:37). Paul was convinced of sin, and so was the Philippian jailer, and so was Augustine, and so was Luther, and so were Hooker, and Pascal, and Bunyan, and Brainerd, and Wesley, and Simeon, and Chalmers – strange collation of names, men in almost every respect dissimilar, but alike in this common characteristic of conviction of sin. And who shall count the examples of the same work, here and now, in our time, in our land, in every land where the gospel of the Son of God has found its way? No law of sex, or age, or temperament, or circumstances, can be traced in the matter; no law but that 'of the Spirit of life in Christ Jesus' (Rom. 8:2).

This convicting whisper and unveiling finds it way to the youngest and to the most aged conscience, to the miserable and to the happy in external conditions, to the savage and to the scholar, to the profligate and to the man who on every standard short of that of God in Christ is, as Saul of Tarsus was, sincerely moral. So I count it altogether likely that my reader is one who can 'set his seal' that the doctrine of individual conviction of sin by the Holy Spirit is true, is true for him. I do not know, I cannot guess, how it has come to him; the manner and method, and occasion. Perhaps, as a matter of biography, it has come not in the first pages of his Christian experience, but later. So Zinzendorf, whose conversion came in the first phase of it through an overpowering insight into the love and loveliness of his Redeemer, was taught not till later the depths of his need of that Redeemer's sacrifice. Perhaps it has come, not as one great critical occasion, one narrow while intense cloud to be passed through, but rather stage

by stage, in intervals and developments of self-discovery.
Or perhaps – and indeed such cases do take place – it was
really the decisive *first* handling of your soul, so far as
you can estimate such facts, by the great regenerator. In
some course of open or hidden rebellion against the light,
or just in the midst of dull or complacent indifference; in
the house of God, in the mission-hall, amidst many
awakened ones, or quite as likely in the walk on the hill-
side or in the street or in your own room at college, or at
home; lo, the Spirit touched you into an insight you had
not even imagined before of sin, and righteousness, and
judgment; of the *necessity* and reality of Christ. And as in
that conviction, soon or slowly, you were led by the same
blessed worker up to the point of simplest acceptance of
your crucified Lord for your Saviour and your King, you
know how the whole colour and texture of subsequent faith
was affected through and through by the initial conviction.
Everything took results from it. Your insight into the
wonder, glory, and virtue of the propitiation; your
submission to the revealed 'indignation and wrath' of the
righteous Judge (Rom. 2:8), and your rejection for ever of
the 'vain words' which try to say that that wrath is not
actually 'coming upon the children of disobedience' (Eph.
5:6); your pity and love for souls as yet entranced in the
sleep from which you have been awakened; all became
what they could not be, without some genuine personal
experience of the Spirit's convincing power.

   You understood now, in the moral sense of
understanding, what is meant by the remark that
'Christianity cannot be proved except to a bad conscience'.
For 'bad' you read 'awakened'; and it is indeed true for
you. The gospel is a message not for man in the abstract,

but for man a sinner. Till you saw yourself to be this latter, under the Spirit's convictions, the gospel was a something for which you seemed to find in yourself no true receptacle, a key which did but rattle, so to speak, in a lock not made exactly for it. Now the Spirit has spoken to your soul of sin; and with a blessed intuition you behold, and believe, the divine provision for your release alike from its guilt and from its power. *Rock of Ages* is a new hymn to the man who is convinced by the Paraclete of sin, righteousness and judgment. And wonderfully now does the Bible open itself to that man, and fall into order and relation before him, and disclose its inner harmonies in his sight. The protoevangelium of Genesis (Gen. 3:15) is no myth to him now, nor are the sacrifices of the Mosaic altar an invention of man. Every type and prophecy is lighted up by its relation to the cross, and in turn lights up the convinced man's apprehension of the cross in the holy details of its ever-blessed significance. And precious indeed to him now is every trace of apostolic doctrine which unfolds the treasures of the accomplished mystery of Calvary. The third chapter of the Romans, and of the Galatians, and the whole teaching of the Hebrews, culminating in 13:20, 21, are dear to him now with a sense of personal companionship and intimacy. So Jesus Crucified, like the celestial bow upon the cloud, manifested as God's antithesis to the manifestation of the guilt of sin. And so is Jesus Risen manifested, as he had not been, as he could not be before, in all the glory of his finished work, and his indwelling and sin-subduing presence (by the same Spirit who has thus convinced the soul), and in all the warmth and radiance of that 'living hope' to which the man is now personally and individually 'begotten again'

(1 Pet. 1:3). And as this richly blessed penitent looks forward to the now dear and happy prospect of the life to come, in the peace and strength of an evidence of its reality as real as it is internal, what is his anticipation? he looks for a world, a life, a work, of sinless bliss, of entire and positive holiness in everlasting personal joy; but he looks to live, love and *serve* there as one who will for ever rejoice (wonderful paradox) to remember that '*when we were sinners, Christ died for us* (Rom. 5:8) and to praise the blessed Name not of an abstract Deity but of 'GOD and of *the Lamb*' (Rev. 7:10).

Was it too bold of the medieval believers to say, '*O beata culpa, quæ talem meruista Redemptorem*'; 'Blessed guilt, which hast won such a Redeemer'?

We need conviction for ourselves as individuals, if our personal religion is to *strike root downward,* and so to bear fruit upward. The man who knows little of conviction of sin, as a genuine element in personal experience, may be many good things, but I do not think he can be a deep Christian.

And greatly do we pastors need this for our ministry. A full, strong current of opinion in the professing church of Christ runs at the present day directly against a grave, thorough-going, doctrine of sin, and its correlative truths of eternal judgment, and of the unspeakable need of the atoning blood, and of living personal faith, in the crucified and risen One, 'according to the Scriptures'. One would think that some even earnest teachers had learned, by some other path surely than that of the Word of God, to look with temperate eyes upon sin, as a phenomenon sure at last to disappear under long processes of divine order; a discord awaiting only its musical resolution; a 'fall upward', perhaps on to some higher level of enriched consciousness.

Let no man deceive us with such vain words. And let us pray that our lips may never pass them on. And to that intent may the Holy Spirit of promise evermore teach us, close to the cross and to the open grave, his lessons of sin, righteousness, and of judgment.

Even so. But from *every other* aspect of the matter we must say, we must cry, the very opposite of *'O beata culpa'*. And we who believe, and who may have been convinced of sin, righteousness and judgment, must humbly and persistently look to the same holy convincer who began the work that he may deepen it and develop it throughout our whole lives, and (let me add to my ministerial brethren) throughout our whole ministry. If in one aspect the conviction of sin is the great initial work of the Spirit, from another aspect it is a work which we can never dare to wish him to wind up here below. Has the believer ever reached the real end of self-discovery? Has he ever really seen with ultimate adequacy how truly his happiest actual obedience 'cannot endure the severity of the *divine judgment'*? Has he ever quite fully realized his need of 'Christ for him'? No, he has not. So now, and tomorrow, and always, we will ask the convincer to carry on in the blessed home of grace the lesson he mercifully began upon the desert sands; to keep us alive and awake, tenderly, humbly, and evermore, to sin, and righteousness, and judgment, in the light, in the blissful light of Christ.

Chapter 6

The Holy Spirit Creating Faith in Jesus

We have endeavoured to think out something of the great subject of conviction of sin by the Spirit of God. Perhaps I should rather say not to think it out, but to think it in; to turn inward in view of it, and question our souls, writer and reader together, about our own insights into the 'exceeding sinfulness of sin' (Rom. 7:13) in the light of the Holy Ghost.

I turn now to the glorious other side of the operation of the Spirit in his work of new creation, re-constitution, of us sinners. I turn to his dealings with us in the way of making our Lord Jesus Christ to be to us what he is given to be to such as we are – our spiritual 'life, and breath, and all things'; our 'righteousness, and sanctification, and redemption' (1 Cor. 1:30); our joy, our peace, our power, our hope. We have seen the heavenly worker ploughing the soil, breaking up the fallow, crushing the underlying rock into dust. We see him now dropping the seed, letting fall the divine 'corn of wheat' into the ground (John 12:24). We see him applying Christ to the sorely needing soul, now conscious of its need. And we see him to this end dealing with it as the Spirit of manifestation, 'revealing in it the Son of God' (Gal. 1:16).

Here is indeed the Holy Spirit's congenial, beloved work. For he is the 'Spirit of Christ'. And in our second chapter we saw how deep the indications of that phrase go; how the Spirit is not only the emissary of Christ, but, in the inner life of Godhead, the stream from him the fountain. Wonderful is the union of nature and of operation so indicated; wonderful, blissful, divinely deep and tender, the union and communion of that love of the Spirit and the Son.

Let us dwell a little on this point of truth. It is possible, and it is not uncommon, so to dwell on the convincing work of the Spirit as to associate his action mainly with that side of grace; as if his *characteristic* were to penetrate, to detect, to expose the soul to itself, to cast it down wounded and broken. But, no, it is not so. I have striven to lay all the emphasis I can on the unspeakable importance of the work of conviction. But therefore I am all the more free to remind my reader and brother that this is after all the Spirit's 'strange work'. The eternal dove, the Spirit of grace, the 'good Spirit' ((Neh. 9:20), has for his *dear and welcome* function the uplifting of the sweet glory of Christ to the aching eyes of the contrite; the applying of the soft balm of Christ to the wounds he himself has mercifully made through 'soul and spirit' (Heb. 4:12).

There is a delightful little book by the late venerable Dr. Horatius Bonar, *The Gospel of the Spirit's Love*. It is only a tract, of less than fifty pages; but it is full of that *theology of consolation* which has few better modern expositors than the deeply taught saints and thinkers trained in the thorough views of our sin and ruin expounded in the Scottish Confession, and in that adoring insight into the wonder, and glory, and tenderness of the work of grace which seems specially given to those who have accepted the whole truth of man's ruin. I commend this little book to my reader. It will press home on him on every side the

conviction that indeed 'Thy Spirit *is good*' (Ps. 143:10);
that the love of the Spirit, as truly as that of the Son,
'passeth knowledge'; that it is a deep mistake, a fallacy
which chills and blights the soul's life, to fail to recognize
this; 'as if there were something in the Spirit which repelled
us, whatever there might be in Christ to attract us; as if the
light which the cross throws upon the love of the Spirit
were not quite in harmony with that which reveals of the
love of Christ, as if the Spirit were not always as ready
with his help as is the Son.' And one passage close to this
short quotation, speaks in words pregnant with truth about
our special subject here, his glorification of Christ to us:

'The want of stable *peace,* of which so many complain, may
arise from imperfect views of the Spirit's love. True, our
peace comes from the one work of the substitute upon the
cross, from the blood of the one sacrifice, from the sin-
bearing of him who has made peace by the blood of the
Cross. But it is the Holy Spirit who glorifies Christ to us,
and takes the scales from our eyes. If, then, we doubt his
love, can we expect him to reveal the Son in our hearts? Are
we not thrusting him away, and hindering that view of the
peace-making which he alone can give?... Perhaps the want
of *faith,* which we often mourn over, may arise from our
not realizing the Spirit's love. "Faith" (no doubt) "cometh
by hearing, and hearing by the word of God"; yet it is the
Holy Spirit who shines upon the word; it is he who gives
the seeing eye and the hearing ear. Under the pressure of
unbelief have we fled to him, and appealed to his love?
"Lord, I believe; help Thou mine unbelief," may be as aptly
a cry to the Spirit as to the Son of God. He helpeth our
infirmities; and in the infirmity of our faith he will most
assuredly succour us. It is through him that we become strong
in faith; and he *loves* to impart the needed strength. He giveth

to all men liberally, and upbraideth not. Yet in our dealings with him regarding faith let us remember that he does not operate in some mystical or miraculous way, as if imparting to us a new faculty called faith; but by taking of the things of Christ and showing them to us; so touching our faculties by his mighty yet invisible hand, that, ere we are aware, these disordered souls of ours begin to work aright, and these dull eyes of ours begin to see what was all along before them, but what they had never perceived, "the excellency of the knowledge of Christ Jesus our Lord".'

So it is the 'loving Spirit' who, having convinced us, testifies of Christ, and glorifies Christ, with the heavenly skill and power of a love as tender, as gentle, as it is divine. He brings the soul down into self-knowledge, into a *know thyself* of the true sort, and then he brings it up into the glorious counterpart, into the knowledge not of a 'better self' but of Jesus Christ, in all the fulness of what he is. And he loves to do it. It is not only his eternally appointed, but surely also his eternally beloved work.

As we pass on, let me call attention to Dr. Bonar's statements quoted just above regarding the Spirit's gift of faith to us, and his mode of giving. My readers well know that it has been a grave question whether the Spirit, whether God, does 'give' faith; whether rather faith is not just that which we have to contribute *of our own store* to the work of conversion. I am indeed aware of the mysteries which connect themselves with that question. But I am quite sure that Scripture does nevertheless teach us that a living and saving faith is as truly a gift of God as is, for instance, 'repentance' (Acts 5:31).

I find this stated in Ephesians 2:8; a passage where, if

the context is attended to, the stress of the argument is all in favour of explaining the words '*and that* not of yourselves, it is the gift of God', to mean that the matter just before mentioned, namely the presence of faith in the saved, is the gift of God. I read the same truth in the phraseology of Philippians 1:29, where alike the power to believe and the call to suffer are seen as 'the gift' given to the saints. And I see it very clearly, in a yet deeper and more suggestive connection, in 2 Corinthians 4:13, where the apostle speaks of himself and his fellow-workers as 'having the same spirit of faith' with the Old Testament saints. I believe the word 'spirit' there to refer to the blessed personal Spirit; but that point is not necessary to the present purpose. What anywise the passage intimates is that faith is not of nature, but of grace. It is from above, not from the resources of human nature; it is the special and supernatural gift of God.

I know the mystery involved, and indeed I feel it; but I entrust it to him who, unlike me, knows the whole eternal case, and will one day gloriously justify those days of grace which he calls us now to trust. And so I hold, and I am sure it is good to hold, that, where a man believes to life eternal, it will be made plain hereafter, if not now, that every link in the chain, not every link except one, was 'mercy from first to last', and very special mercy too.

But then on the other hand this view of the gift of faith, as Dr. Bonar well puts it, does not for a moment lead us to think of faith as of an alien or exotic something inserted, like a life-germ from another planet, into our nature. 'Faith is trust,' say what the Council of Trent[1] may. Our Lord's

---

1. In the *Canons and Decrees of the Council of Trent*, c. ix. of Session vi. is devoted to the 'refutation' of the *inanis hæretico-rum fiducia;*

use of the word πιστις in the Gospels proves this. Faith is trust, reliance, personal confidence. And personal confidence, self-entrustment to another, is in itself a perfectly *natural* exercise of the human soul. What then is *super*natural, what is divine gift, about it in this great instance of saving faith? Why, surely, just that which can be illustrated from the experiences of human life, whenever anything 'gives me confidence' in another. In such a case, the fact of my need being presupposed, and the fact of my consciousness of my need – the fact, for instance, of my knowing myself to be very ill – what 'gives me confidence' in such or such a physician? The convincing manifestation to me of his personal trustworthiness. Suppose me full conscious of my urgent need of a physician, with a consciousness so strong that *ipso facto* I am willing to use a physician, and suppose the trustworthiness of that particular man manifested to me by good proofs; there is thus and then 'given' to me the gift of faith in him.

Transfer this to the case of (not anyone but) the awakened sinner. The Spirit has convinced him of his need – deep, wide, and urgent – of salvation. The Spirit now 'takes of the things of Christ, and shows them to' the soul thus prepared to behold them to purpose (John 16:15). The Lord and Saviour, in his fitness, his adequacy, his unspeakable trustworthiness, stands before it. The need, divinely shown, is met by the response and the supply, divine and shown divinely; and the man lays his hand, sets his foot, upon the Rock, because it is wanted and because it is there. He entrusts himself to his manifested

---

and Canon xii of the Session anathematizes those who say *fidem justificantem nihil aliud esse quam fiduciam divinæ misericordiæ, peccata remittentis propter Christum.*

Saviour, and is his. He believes, and it is with a faith that is the gift of God.

It is important, if I understand the case at all, to remember clearly in this whole matter what in it is natural and what is supernatural. The natural element is the action of a human soul, conscious of exceeding need, accepting the perfect provision for that need, seen to be such. And from this point of view it is the preacher's, and the private friend's, blessed privilege and duty to point the awakened person as directly, simply and practically as possible to the facts of the Lord Jesus Christ's person, work, willingness, love. No considerations of the supernatural ought for a moment to disturb that action, any more than if we were concerned in recommending a tried physician to a friend in illness.

Only today it has been my duty and my blessing to try to deal thus with a wearied and burdened mind and soul; and my steady aim was, secretly indeed to invoke the Spirit's grace, but also to point out in the simplest and most practical terms the 'reason of the hope that is in us' (1 Pet. 3:15); the central certainty of the resurrection of the buried Lord of Calvary, and the light (amidst whatever surrounding darkness) which that one precious fact sheds upon all he did, and said, and is. And with the effort to state the 'reason of the hope' it was inevitable also to bear personal witness to the experienced reality of its power, the experienced mercy and love of this risen Saviour, and thus to bring in the forces, so far as possible, of the sympathy of soul with soul.

All this was, from one point of view, a natural proceeding; as natural as if I had been asserting and justifying my recommendation, on grounds of common

reason and experience, of some medical or legal adviser
of whose aid my friend stood in need. But all the while I
knew full well that 'God must give the increase' (1 Cor.
3:6), God the Holy Spirit. I had a bright hope that he would
use my poor reasonings and witness in order to bring the
soul of my friend (who is very little likely ever to read
these words) to a saving view of Jesus Christ; or that
anywise he would *somehow* cause the *reason* of the gospel
to present itself satisfactorily *to* his mind.

But well I knew that there needed also, in order to that
man's believing unto life eternal, a special dealing by the
Holy Ghost with those materials of argument and witness.
It was needful that he, divine and personal, should speak
in ways in which I cannot, and no man can, to the depths
of that spirit about 'this same Jesus'; should 'testify of
him' and 'glorify him' (John 15:26; 16:14), as no man can,
to that human consciousness. He must in his own way
make facts more then mere facts, the witness more than
just credible, the Lord more than an assured certainty of the
past, or of the unseen present; even the ineffably attractive
magnet, desire, repose, of this burdened soul. The mystery
of the Fall is a fact. Man's spirit does not of itself 'see
beauty in him that it should desire him', (though no act of
inward seeing is more absolutely reasonable,) until 'the
Spirit of the Lord' gives that 'liberty' (2 Cor. 3:17, 18)
which comes along with a new grace-given intuition into
'the glory of God in the face of Jesus Christ' (2 Cor. 4:6).

Thus, naturally at once and supernaturally, the blessed
Spirit 'gives faith' in Jesus. Naturally, by providing that
the facts about him, and his work, and his love, shall come
in some genuine measure before the mental eyes.
Supernaturally, by bringing the soul, fallen from that

original righteousness in which it was in sympathy and harmony with God, back into sympathy with the blessed facts. And this he does in part through his work of conviction of sin, and in part through shedding upon 'the truth as it is in Jesus' (Eph. 4:21), in ways wholly of his own, a light of glory and beauty, or however of *reality,* which 'eye hath not seen' (1 Cor. 2:9, 10), but which 'God revealeth by his Spirit'. And so the soul sees, and the man believes and comes, entrusting himself to the divinely manifested Christ, and 'believing, hath life through his Name' (John 20:31).

It is most true that saving faith is not always so given as that the *order of the process* of its giving can be described just as above. There are conversions where the process is, in a certain sense, reversed. Such a conversion was that of Count Zinzendorf, the second founder of the 'Moravian' Church, the *Unitas Fratum,* with its marvellous missionary enterprises.[2] His new birth to righteousness and God was wrought, so the story runs, through the sight of a picture of the crucifixion, bearing the inscription, '*This have I done for thee; what has thou done for me?*' He

---

2. Since writing this passage I have examined Bishop Spangenberg's *Life of Zinzendorf,* which as the work of the Count's intimate Christian friend is the best authority on such a subject as this. And I do not find all the statements in my text quite borne out. The narrative runs thus (p. 15): 'From [Frankfort-on-the-Main] they proceeded to Düsseldorf, where the Count's attention was particularly attracted by the excellent *Ecce Homo* in the picture-gallery, under which was the following inscription: "All this I have done for thee; what doest thou for Me?" He reflected that he would scarcely be able to answer this question, and besought his Saviour to force him into the fellowship of his sufferings, if he should ever be disinclined to it.' he was just nineteen at the time; and his own account of his earlier years makes it plain

gazed, loved, and rejoiced 'with exceeding joy', turning from a life of indecision at once, and without a pang, to Christ. But do not think that the element of conviction was absent in Zinzendorf's experience as a whole. It came later, and with power. And it was an element most necessary, as his life-story shows, in order to save him from some grave wanderings from sound faith in the matter of Christian experience, and from a tendency to drift away from a steady anchorage on the atoning work of the Lamb of God. And I am well assured that that after-gift of spiritual conviction tended in its turn only to deepen and develop for Zinzendorf the first gift of joy and love. The elements which we have dwelt upon as characteristic of conversion and its life were there, though the order of their arrival, if I may call it so, was abnormal. His faith in its

---

that he both was, and knew himself to be, a believer long before that time. 'It was my happiness early to experience a heartfelt impression of the Saviour; after this all my wishes and desires were directed towards the Bridegroom of my soul, that I might live unto him who atoned for me' (p.3). But something not wholly unlike the account given in the text is alluded to in another extract (p.4) from his own words: 'I was told [as a child] concerning my Creator, that he became a man.... I felt happy in conversing with him, and grateful for his having remembered me for good in his Incarnation. But I did not fully understand the greatness and sufficiency of his meritorious sufferings, nor was my own wretchedness and inability sufficiently obvious to me. I did also what I could in order to be saved, *until one extraordinary day,* when I was so much affected by what my Creator had suffered for me that I shed an abundance of tears, and attached and joined myself still more closely to him.'

On the whole I have preferred to leave the text as it stands, with this note. The experience, which without quite adequate evidence is assigned in it to Zinzendorf, is however an experience realized in many instances.

sum total was the repose of the divinely awakened soul in
the divinely manifested Saviour.

I appealed in my last chapter to my reader's own
experience. May I do so again in this brighter and more
blessed connection? In anything but an inquisitorial spirit,
I do venture to say to you, has the Holy Spirit testified to
you of Jesus Christ, glorified to you Jesus Christ, taking
of his things and showing them unto you? I do not ask,
have you had this vivid crisis of consciousness, that almost
vision of the unseen and eternal? I am not one of those
who speak lightly of such things, as if they were to be
estimated off-hand as so many illusions, a discredit to sober
faith. Faith is magnificently sober as to its grounds, and
as to its nature. But when we remember that what it clasps
is *Jesus Christ*, and what it receives is the life eternal and
the hope of glory, shall we think it necessarily fanaticism
if sometimes, and in some Christians, 'the sweet unveilings
of his face' have been such as even to agitate greatly the
faculties of the mortal tabernacle?

'My earthly by his heavenly overpower'd
Sank down.'

But I do not speak to you now of these things, which
certainly are not the *daily* 'bread of life'. I only ask, has
the Lord Jesus Christ been so 'revealed in you' that it is
no forced figure of speech to say that he has been
'glorified'?

Has he been so shown to the eyesight of the inner man
as the Lamb of Calvary that you not only hold (as it is so
good to hold) the clearest mental convictions about

justification by faith, but that the Crucified, the shedder of the justifying blood, is *the adored and beloved* of your awakened and confiding soul?

Has he been so shown within you as the Son of the Father, the Only Begotten in the Father's bosom, that you not only reject with fullest intellectual conviction the misbeliefs of a Sabellius, an Arius, or a Socinus, in their oldest or their most modern phases, but that your spirit does indeed 'kiss the Son' (Ps. 2:12) with the deepest homage of worshipping love, responding in sweet harmony to the voice out of the bright cloud – 'This is *my beloved* Son?' (Matt. 17:5).

Has he so shown within you as your sovereign Master that you not only reasonably own his claims but find that a complete submission to them is pure happiness, because it is so real a means to *feeling the bond* which unites you for ever to him?

Has he been so shown within you as your life, your power, your wealth of resource against the devil, the world, and the flesh, and your enablement for humble service to his will, that you not only applaud a spiritual theory, and take pleasure in its exposition, but '*take pleasure in infirmities,* that the power of Christ may rest upon you' (2 Cor. 12:9), and his beloved presence be felt as it hardly can be felt without the cross?

Is it thus with you? Is it not thus with you? It is a divine reality, is it not? Calm and pure in its holy essence, this glorification of Christ yet moves and thrills with a 'joy unspeakable and full of glory' (1 Pet. 1:8). And it is the Holy Spirit to whom immediately the thanks for that joy are due. You, convinced and believing soul, reaping these fruits of living faith in the Son of God, are a subject of the

best-beloved work of the loving Spirit. His breath has
moved the cloud for you from the face of eternal Beauty,
and has quickened you into the consciousness of what it
is. 'HE hath been thus effectual in this secret work of your
regeneration unto newness of life'; in this new birth 'unto
a living hope' (1 Pet. 1:3).

Love him, adore him, give thanks to him. And
meanwhile seek and expect his abiding and continuous
work of loving grace. Look up to the Father, in this as in
so many other spiritual connections, with the prayer, sure
to be answered, 'Take not thy Holy Spirit from me' (Ps.
51:11). Expect, and humbly receive, not only an ever
deeper view of the sinfulness of sin, but also an ever deeper
view of the glory of Christ, seen in the secret places of
present communion with him and obedience to him. The
Spirit will unfold more to you, and yet more, of 'the
unsearchable riches' (Eph. 3:8) and their applications. He
will 'strengthen you in the inner man', so that 'Christ shall
dwell in your heart by faith' with a blessed development
of continuousness and power, and so that you shall 'know
the love of Christ' (Eph. 3:16, 17, 19), with the joy of an
ever new discovery.

'Come Holy Spirit, come,
Let thy bright beams arise;
Dispel the darkness from our minds
And open all our eyes.

'Convince us of our sin,
Then lead to Jesu's blood,
And to our wondering view reveal   .
The secret love of God.

'Show us that loving Man
That rules the courts of bliss,
The Lord of Hosts, the mighty God,
The eternal Prince of Peace.

'Tis thine to cleanse the heart,
To sanctify the soul,
To put fresh life in every part
And new-create the whole.

'Dwell, therefore, in our hearts,
Our minds from bondage free;
Then we shall know, and praise, and love,
The Father, Son, and thee.'

So, many years ago, wrote Joseph Hart; and the need, the promise, and the prayer are the same this day.

Chapter 7

The Holy Spirit and
the Believer's New Life (1)

We have considered now, in our view of the revelation through John of the Holy Spirit's work, three main passages dealing with that work. We have seen the Spirit as our regenerator from spiritual death into spiritual life, and as our convincer (John 3), and as the glorifier of Christ in the souls of the convinced (John 16). In this study we have looked from different points of view upon his supremely important function and action in bringing the individual into that living union with the Son of God of which we treated in a previous chapter. That union, as we there remembered, is altogether by the Holy Spirit, and is normally effected by him through the processes of repentance and faith, under which the man lays hold of and receives him who is our life, and receives in him all his blessed fulness, the 'grace for grace' (John 1:16) of a perpetual and ever-new supply of the peace and power which is in Christ

We have thus as it were seen the soul safe arrived at its union with the Lord; and now henceforth its life, the whole life of the man thus united, is to be a new life, a spiritual life, a perpetual reception out of Christ following upon that initial entrance into him. How then is this life to be led? Is the man now to take his spiritual affairs into his own hands? Has the Spirit led him up to his Redeemer, and there left him? No, most certainly. True it is that the experiences of this new life are to be as personal, as conscious, as truly voluntary (let us not forget this), as those of the old. 'No will is so fully equipped for work as the regenerate will.' The whole Scripture overflows with illustrations and reminders of that fact. Nevertheless the new life, if the man is living it indeed, is to have in it from first to last this divine and glorious new factor, the inworking presence of the blessed personal Paraclete, who in a sense now new and special is both to guard and animate the 'first springs of thought and will', and above all to keep alive, by continuous application of Christ, the life he gave by first application of Christ. Thus, in the words of a hymn dear to many a believing heart,

'Every virtue we possess,
   And every victory won,
And every thought of holiness,
   Are his alone.'

Following our proposed method of Scripture study, I keep still to the Gospel according to John, reserving for after study the forms of truth given through Paul. And to illustrate from John the work of the Spirit in the developing experience of the regenerate believer, I go again to the same Paschal Discourse of our beloved Lord which we have approached in the two previous chapters. We have found there his own account of some initial steps in the Spirit's saving work. We shall now find there, in the words of the same Teacher, a delineation of some of the inmost characteristics of the true life of his true followers, such as it was already in a measure then, and such as it soon was to become in rich development under the developed inworking of the Spirit.

In this whole delineation we have to remember that
although the Holy Spirit is only occasionally mentioned
he is everywhere implied. For the discourse of the whole
manifestly deals with the disciples' experience in view of
the withdrawal of the bodily presence of Jesus Christ. And
the promised equivalent, and more than equivalent, for
that presence was to be the developed presence of the
Comforter. As therefore the whole previous walk and life
of the disciples had been bound up with the presence and
power of their dear visible Master, so now their whole
walk and life was to be bound up, in a connection as
necessary, tender and powerful as possible, with the
presence in them of this his holy representative; by whom
already they had come to believe on the name of the Son
of God and to be, however little they understood it as yet,
united to him in the eternal life. We read then rightly all
through the discourse, and all through the High Priestly
prayer at its close, the underlying truth of the work of the
Spirit, effecting every blessed experience in the whole new
life of the disciple.

And here let me point out the rightness of referring
these promises of the Paschal Chamber not to the apostles
only but to us, to every member of the believing church.
There are, I doubt not, words in the discourse and the prayer
which have a primary reference to the apostles, and to
their past and present experience, and to their coming work
as the Spirit-taught, infallible teachers of the church. But
there are indications everywhere that the apostles then, as
on many another occasion, were viewed by the Lord Jesus
not only as guides and teachers of the church, but as 'the
church by representation', if I may use the phrase. In the
fourteenth chapter, for example, we find our Lord

continually passing from words bearing a primary special reference to the apostles to words completely inclusive in their terms. 'He that believeth on me, the works that I do shall he do also' (ver. 12); 'he that hath my commandments and keepeth them ... I will manifest myself to him' (ver. 21); 'If a man love me ... we will make our abode with him' (ver. 23). And indeed all through the great passage, with hardly an exception, we feel that it is rather the *Christian* life and character than specially the *apostolic* that is in view; the same life and character which the First Epistle of John depicts and explains without any reference at all to special ministerial functions assigned to any sharers in it. So without hesitation or reserve I read these precious words of the Lord Jesus, spoken on the eve of his death and glory, as on the one hand bearing throughout on the work of the Spirit, and on the other hand applicable throughout to the life, needs, privileges and possibilities of every true believer. With these principles in mind let us come to the study.

I read then first in this discourse some divine revelations about the oneness of the saints with Christ, and with the Father, and so with one another. 'At that day' (the day surely of the promised coming of the Comforter), 'ye shall know that I am in my Father, and ye in me, and I in you' (John 14:20); 'That they all may be one; as thou, Father, art in me, and I in thee, that they also may be one in us'; 'And the glory which thou gavest me I have given them; that they may be one, even as we are one; I in them, and thou in me, that they may be made perfect in one'; 'And I have declared unto them thy name, and will declare it; that the love wherewith, thou hast loved me may be in them, and I in them' (John 17:21, 22, 23, 26). Ponder the words, as if you had never read them before.

I well remember an occasion when they were thus brought forcibly and anew to my mind. It was an anxious hour of public religious discussion on the nature of the divine life in the Christian. One deeply-earnest speaker carried his statements to a length which in my view was, as it still is, at variance with the holy proportion of revealed truth; leading through truth out of truth to a related error which lay beyond it. But God sometimes overrules even a manifest exaggeration or distortion to call attention to something which it distorts but which we, perhaps, have neglected and ignored. So it was with me then. The solemnity, the intense significance, the pregnant emphasis, with which my friend and opponent that day repeated the words of John 14:20: 'At that day ye shall know that I am in the Father, and ye in me, and I in you', sank deep into one heart at least of those present and asked it whether there did not lie in these words treasures of grace as yet unsuspected and unclaimed; and so there did.

May I again, as I have done more than once before, turn to my reader and ask if perhaps it is so now with him? And if so, may I in my turn entreat him to listen to those divine words in the silence of the soul, as to a revelation of principles and powers and experiences and possibilities which have not the remotest necessary connection with fanaticism but which may nevertheless *mean* an inner life far different from a life of fitful and intermittent faith, love, joy, peace, and power for witness-bearing and light-bearing for Christ?

The verses cited above from the seventeenth chapter have, I well know, a momentous bearing on questions of church unity, and are a standing caution of the utmost gravity and tenderness against the spirit and schismatic separation and antagonism in external Christian life. But while remembering this, and reminding my reader of it, I must yet more earnestly point out that the inner and intense meaning of the words has to do with regions of truth, life, and experience compared with which even the sacred and important truths of exterior church unity are a lower region.

It has to do primarily with the vital, spiritual, eternal union of 'the church of the firstborn written in heaven' (Heb. 12:23) with their glorious Head, union in a life which is altogether of God in its root and fruit. It has to do with 'knowledge' and experiences to which 'the world' is an utter stranger, with insights into everlasting love and joy coming down from the Father of Lights, and with a cohesion and co-operation, a united work and witness, which depend absolutely for their possibility and power on the recognition and following out of *such* principles of union.

Blessed will it be for the church and for the world when these principles shall so vastly prevail as to find expression naturally and from within in a harmonious counterpart of order; a far different thing from what it is, I cannot but think, an illusory prospect – the attainment of such internal unity by a previous exaction of exterior governmental uniformity.

But this is by the way. My point is now to call attention to the wonderful depth and height, and personally searching and alluring power, of these words of the Lord about oneness, and then to remind my reader that the realization of those words lies in the work of the Holy Spirit. It is as HE unites me, and unites thee, to Christ, by his new-creating and life-giving touch and drawing, that

we enter into this amazing oneness with the Son, and the
Father, and one another; a oneness spiritually organic, in
which each personality, while quite exempt from *invasion*,
falls under the power of a divine *cohesion* whose results
in spiritual harmony of life and action will develop for
ever. 'These things worketh that one and the selfsame
Spirit,' blessed be his Name.

Along with this revelation of spiritual and Spirit-
wrought oneness between the believer and the Lord, and
between believers in the Lord, I gather up from this same
discourse many another precious kindred word. There is
that great promise, 'Because I live, ye shall live also' (John
14:19). It is a promise not merely of the Rescuer to the
rescued, of the Saviour to the saved, of the Leader to the
led, of the Head to the limb, of the Vine to the branch. We
rest on that promise, we humbly believe it. 'Looking off
unto Jesus' (Heb. 12:2, very definitely and very
necessarily, '*off* unto' him), we appropriate it, and take it
for granted, and act on it amidst the realities of life. 'When
thronging duties press,' when by the providence of God
we have to meet men, to walk up and down in the world
of the present day, we yet fall back internally on the truth
that 'he that hath the Son hath life' (1 John 5:12). The
basis of our true being, the spring-head of our true life-
pulse, is in him. Even so; and therefore, while he liveth,
and because he liveth, we 'shall not die but live'. And this
too 'spake he of the Spirit'. The Worker of this our abiding
life is 'the Lord, the Life-giver', the giver to us in inward
reality of the Son who is our life.[4] And shall we not bless
his Name?

Closely in the same connection I read here of blessed
articulate experiences and realizations of this union and

life. I read of 'union turned into communion'. I listen to the Son of God speaking not only to John and to Peter, but to me, that Paschal evening; and I hear him say, 'I will not leave you orphans; I will come to you'; 'The world seeth me no more, but ye see me' (John 14:18, 19); 'I will see you again, and your hearts shall rejoice' (John 16:22); 'I will manifest myself to him' (John 14:21); 'My Father will love him, and we will come unto him, and make our abode with him' (John 14:22-23). I read these promises, coming direct from the lips of our Lord, and life, and I remember along with them those other words which he spoke out of his glorified life through this same John : 'To him that overcometh I will give to eat of the hidden manna' (Rev. 2:17); 'I will come in to him, and will sup with him, and he with Me' (Rev. 3:20). And we bless him for even the least realization of what they mean. And we remember that it is the Holy Spirit who brings about these realizations in us, who gives us to know in any measure what is meant by the indwelling and overshadowing of Jesus Christ. And as we possess and enjoy this wonderful, this infinitely merciful gift of the known presence of the Son of God, and of the Father in him, we thank and adore the personal and gracious Holy Spirit that is thus with the soul.

'Shall I ever forget the summer morning, in 1886,' writes one whom I know, 'when on the sunny slopes of a Yorkshire moor, on a brief holiday, not long after that blessed time of spiritual discovery and strengthening in the knowledge of God, I experienced indeed a "joy unspeakable and full of glory" in the sight of our Lord and Life? Walking out alone I fell into prayer, prayer to be conformed in all things to the will of him who had redeemed me and drawn me to himself. As I proceeded, while heart and mind were kept in the deepest peace, and not the slightest enthusiastic disturbance of judgment was to be suspected, it was yet as if a heaven were opened around me, and the joy of the Lord flowed in divine effusion over my being. The glory and beauty of my Saviour's person, the indescribable reality of his presence both in me and around me, and the absolute "all-sufficiency" of his grace and power, the loveliness and attraction of his "perfect will" – all shone upon me with a brightness of which the August sunshine seemed but a type and a shadow. "The Lord is my portion," said the inmost spirit in that holy hour. In a sense, the glory passed away, as to special excitation. But in a sense, in a yet deeper sense, it abode, diffused among the experiences of life, and proving its "sober certainty of waking bliss" by its power and amidst these experiences, to calm, and purify, and lift above the selfishness of the old life.' And 'all this worked that one and the selfsame Spirit.' It is by him that we 'know the only true God, and Jesus Christ whom he hath sent' (John 17:3), with that knowledge which is no mere result of information and inference mentally collected. It is 'eternal life'. Shall we not bless the Spirit's Name that thus we know?

And so I may go on through the Paschal Discourse. I may take the Lord's words about the True Vine (John 15:1-8), and the branches which are in him, and which abide or remain in him, and by virtue of their conjunction and abiding bring forth fruit; and under this whole paragraph I may read the presence and work of the uniting and life-giving Holy Spirit. To deviate for a moment to Paul, and to a passage with which we shall deal later, we recollect that the sweet fruit of holiness in the disciples's life is 'the fruit *of the Spirit'* (Gal. 5:22). He it is who so works in the man that, having 'come to Christ' and 'received him' (John 1:12; 6:37), he also abides in him as the days and years go on. The man freely and truly 'chooses life' (Deut. 30:19), welcomes and cherishes his Lord's precious indwelling presence and power; but that he freely does so is the gift of the Holy Ghost. Because of him, present and inworking, the man 'abides in the love' of his Lord, and in his friendship, and in his peace (John 10:27; 15:9, 15), and responds with full joy to his joy (John 16:33).

And again, how much we have here about the work and life of *prayer*! 'Whatsoever ye shall ask in my name that will I do'; 'If ye ask anything in my name, I will do it'; 'Ask and ye shall receive, that your joy may be full'; 'I have ordained you, that ye should go and bring forth fruit, and that your fruit should remain; that whatsoever ye shall ask of the Father in my name, he may give it you' (John 14:13, 14; 15:16; 16:24). In those last words we have surely an indication of the deep, vital connection between true prayer and true fruit-bearing; such that the two things are, as it were, convertible terms. It is as if he said, 'I have ordained you to produce real and lasting spiritual effects for me; *in other words*, I have ordained you to be, in me, prevailing petitioners with my Father, that you may be bearers of such fruit.' The 'things asked of the Father in Christ's name' are that the disciple may be a vessel meet for the Master's use, a branch pregnant with holy fruit; and there is therefore a deep and living correspondence between the bearing and the asking. Now here again is the operation of the Spirit, 'the Spirit of grace and of supplications' (Zech. 12:10). The prayer here meant is no mere devout performance of duty, the due utterance of an expression of reverence and independence; it is 'prayer in the Holy Ghost' (Jude 20), who 'maketh intercession for us ... *according to (the will of) God*' (Rom. 8:26, 27). It is a prayer of a heart filled with him, and therefore filled with the humble but intense desire that his will may be done, and in particular that his implement may be used for his glory. Results of life, word, and work in answer to such prayer are 'fruit that remaineth'. And indeed it is the 'fruit of the Spirit'.

I write close to the tenth anniversary of the blessed death of that truly sanctified servant of God, the late Miss Frances Havergal. Her life and work has just now been much in mind, with its rich lesson and holy example. Speaking not for myself only but assuredly for a multitude of other readers, I may truly say that I never read her words of witness for our Lord without a sense of peculiar spiritual weight, influence, and holy persuasion, coming from those words to my heart. In a very marked manner her fruit seems to me to 'remain'; the personal warmth and emphasis of her testimony 'remains', as if the page had a living voice. And for my part I attribute this to the fact that while that devoted Christian was kept by the Spirit of God remarkably loyal to the foundation truths of the ancient and only gospel of grace, she was by the same Spirit led to, and kept in, an attitude of unreserved self-consecration to the Holy Master's work and will which characterize her every effort, literary or otherwise, in his service. By the Spirit she asked to be fruitful, and by the Spirit she bore fruit indeed, 'fruit that remaineth', and shall remain. In our measure, as we too are 'vessels of the Lord', let it be likewise with us, by the same secret.

Is it not somewhere in this direction that the humble

Christian may look for God's fulfilment, in his own way, of that mysterious promise, 'Greater works than these shall he do?' (John 14:12). Very possibly these words bear in their ultimate meaning not so much on the personal work of the individual Christian as on that of the Christian *as a member of* the body and bride of Christ; as if to say, 'he shall have a real, living, full share in that wonderful work of ingathering and upbuilding which I his Master did but "begin" (Acts 1:1), leaving it to my Bride to do more in *that kind* than I had done' (see Col. 1:24). But such a view of the passage can only be true if it leaves clear the fact that wonderful possibilities of fruitful service are open, in the life of the Spirit, to the individual disciple who by the Spirit really lives and walks as a servant and implement of Christ.

Another class of passages in this divine discourse bears explicitly upon the *teaching* work of the Holy Spirit (John 14:26; 16:13; 17:7). Here, I willingly and reverently own, we have a plain primary reference to the special knowledge and authoritative, infallible teaching of the inspired apostles. But I do not think the words can be wholly limited to them. An instructive parallel is 1 John 2:20, 27, where an inspired apostle is addressing all the 'little children' of his flock, and reminding them of their heavenly 'unction', and of its mysterious power to give supernatural knowledge. And I gather from that passage that the true disciple is promised, not apostolic infallibility, but a more than natural instinct in the use of divine revelation, to discern between essential error and essential truth in the things of salvation; a divinely given *feeling,* if I may put it so, for the sound word and against the illusory, counterfeiting substitute for it; and that this is the gift, the presence, the light, of the Holy Spirit in the soul regenerated by him. Like many other great promises it needs to be read side by side with complementary and cautionary truths; but it is there, it is a reality, it is never to be forgotten, it is to be welcomed and used. And the holy Worker is to be blessed and thanked.

In closing I point to those precious words of the High Priestly prayer which speak of the 'keeping' and the 'sanctifying' of the disciples by the Father, who has given them eternal life in the Son; 'Holy Father, keep in thine own name those whom thou has given me, that they may be one, as we are'; 'I pray not that thou shouldest take them out of the world, but that thou shouldest keep them from the evil'; 'Sanctify them in thy truth; thy word is truth' (John 17:11, 15, 17). Need we elaborately explain that here the Spirit's work is to be seen, though his name is not named? How in fact was this prayer of the Son answered in the life and history of the church by the children of God? It was by the effusion of the Spirit, by whom, in a sense and mode so large and full that it was more than compensation for the seen presence of the Son, the true members and the true body were 'governed and sanctified' in the new, wonderful life of the gospel. By him they possessed, and possess, the Father and the Son. By him, the Spirit of faith, they were, and are, 'kept through faith unto salvation' (1 Pet. 1:5), 'Praying in him', they 'keep themselves in the love of God' (Jude 20, 21). Of the Father, through the Son, by the Spirit, comes all keeping power, all sanctifying, separating, consecrating grace. Let us adore the three-fold work; and now specially let us not forget, in our love and praise, the third and immediate blessed Worker.

So we leave the Upper Chamber. Or rather so we close our enquiry into what was said there by the Lord Jesus about the life which is to be lived by us in the Spirit, only we may now and always 'there continually dwell'. Amidst the stress and fulness of life and duty, amidst the realities of trial and temptation, there may we dwell indeed, in internal recollection and experience, 'sitting at the table[1] with' our beloved Lord (John 12:2), leaning upon his sacred breast, and listening to his voice as he teaches us how to live that life of union, abiding, prayer, fruitfulness, spiritual insight, all under divine safe-keeping, which is laid up for those who by the Spirit are indeed 'in Christ, a new creation' (2 Cor. 5:17).

---

1. I need not point out in detail how large and rich, in the light of the truths we have here considered, should be our fruition of our life in Christ by the Spirit when we assemble at *The Lord's Table*, the Table of the Paschal Chamber, at the Lord's most loving command. Not that I limit for a moment the phrase in the text to Eucharistic occasions. Faith and love can turn *our social table* into 'God's board' in a true sense; for certainly they can create a sanctuary in all the places and events of life.

Chapter 8

The Holy Spirit
and the Believer's New Life (2)

The revelation through John of the person and work of the Holy Spirit has now for some time occupied us. We go once more to the same great apostle, before turning, as we shall then do, to the 'beloved brother Paul'.

In John's Gospel there remain two passages in which the Holy Ghost is explicitly mentioned by the Lord Jesus, and whose messages to the believer, and to the believing church, are of the weightiest import. In the First Epistle we have some few further precious contributions of truth on the Spirit's work. In the Revelation finally we have him repeatedly presented, in his heavenly glory and in his work for men. Let us make this a chapter of fragments, taking up these successive passages each for brief remark and meditation.

(1) **John 7:37-39**. Here stands the Saviour before us – 'in the last day, that great day of the feast', the joyous Tabernacle Feast of Autumn, following with significant closeness on the Day of Atonement. The occasion must have been a scene impressive indeed in its externals.

'After the priest had returned from Siloam with his golden pitcher, and for the last time poured its contents to the base of the altar; after the "Hallel" had been sung to the sound of the flute, and people responding and worshipping as the priests three times drew the threefold blasts from their silver trumpets – just when the interest of the people had been raised to its highest pitch, [it was then] that from amidst the mass of worshippers, who were waving towards the altar quite a forest of leafy branches as the last words of Psalm 117 were chanted – a voice was raised, which resounded through the Temple.... It was Jesus, who "stood and cried, saying, If any man thirst, let him come unto Me, and drink". Then by faith in him should each one truly become like the Pool of Siloam, and from his inmost being "rivers of living water flow".... That effect was instantaneous .... Even the Temple guard ... owned the spell of his words, and dared not to lay hands on him. "Never man spake like this man", was the only account they could give of their unusual weakness.'[1]

It was a voice mighty with the power at once of authority and promise. Above and through the mighty maze of symbolism it called the soul of man directly, without one intermediary film or interval, to 'come to' HIM who spoke, to come with an absolute and therefore perfectly simple faith to HIM. And it promised, it guaranteed, with self-evidencing majesty, that to all and several who should so come the very amplest blessing should result. The river of life eternal should so flow into them from Jesus Christ as to flow through them to others. 'As the Scripture had said,' – such Scriptures as Isaiah 12:2, 3 (observe the connection of those verses) and 58:11, – 'out of the belly' of each such believing man 'should flow rivers of living water'.

We are at once informed by the evangelist of the meaning of the glorious imagery: 'This spake he *of the Spirit,* which they that believe on him should receive.' The reference was to the Holy Ghost, in his soon-coming

1. Dr. A. Edersheim, *The Temple and its Services,* p.244.

development of presence and operation in the believing church; 'for the Holy Ghost was not yet [given], because that Jesus was not yet glorified.' Not, surely, that no rich and redundant blessing would have resulted then and there to each believer who took the Saviour at his word that hour; but that in the great order of God's ways such redundancy was not quite yet to be the rule, the open and manifest usage of grace. For must we not observe that, although the fullest allowance is to be made for large and bright exceptions, there was just the difference of *rule* between the spiritual conditions of the old dispensation and the new – that while the old was a dispensation of conservation, the new is a dispensation also, and in wonderful prominence, of diffusion and impartation through the new Israel and through the new Israelite? To a degree altogether unprecedented this began to be at Pentecost. The church, and the saint, were then so filled from above that it was manifestly the purpose of the Lord that not now and then only, and in exceptional cases only, but all the true people of God always should be open channels of blessing to men around, conduits of life, by becoming living vehicles for a living witness to the glory and all-gracious power of Christ.

What Abraham, and David, and Josiah, and Ezra, as regards their personal life and its rule, were *not* altogether meant to be, the whole company of believers, each and all, were altogether meant to be now; channels of effusion and diffusion for the parched and weary world, in which they were to live as men filled with the Spirit who manifests and imparts the Lord.

Much might be said of course on questions in detail which gather around this great truth and principle. We might turn aside to discuss the question of the 'miraculous gifts', and whether they are at all in view here. I think they are not, for I think that here, as in the parallel passage of the Well of Sychar, the very tone and accent, so to speak, of the words of Jesus Christ lead us straight to the needs of the inmost human soul, and to the supply of those needs (John 4:14). And those are needs which, be it said with reverence, would be poorly met indeed by even 'unknown tongues' and 'gifts of healing'. But I will not enter on any details of such a question here. We may be certain that, whatever else lies in these divine words, *this* lies in them – the assurance that the believer, the believer indeed, drawing the depth and fulness of the divine life from Christ by the Spirit, shall in his wholly subordinate way, yet in a way most real, be wonderfully used in the conveyance of that life around him. He shall not be an original fountainhead; only One can be that. But he shall be a *living watercourse;* a living secondary cause in others of living faith, and hope, and love, by the Holy Ghost. He shall not merely speak truth about Christ and the Spirit; he shall speak it as living by it, as living it; he shall speak by 'the power that worketh in him' (Eph. 3:20); he shall touch his brother's conscience, and will, and love, with a contact whose power is not of himself while yet it comes through him.

If I may quote my own words written elsewhere, the Lord 'will use the man, or the woman, who is really drinking the heavenly water from the Rock, who is really filled for life's needs with the supplies of life eternal, in a mysterious way, and yet a way all the while profoundly natural. Through that personality the Spirit shall be pleased to work special blessings, for he will have made it fit to be so used.... It "shall be a vessel unto honour, *sanctified and serviceable to the Master*" (2 Tim. 2:21). The believer in question may perhaps *know* that he is thus privileged and employed, or he may never know it at all. But that matters comparatively little.' What matters is the promise of the all-faithful Lord that we, even we, shall somehow be channels for the life giving operation of the eternal Spirit, on condition that we 'come unto him', for ourselves, 'and drink', and that we live 'believing', live by faith in the Son of God.

Blessed be he, for such a promise, for such a condition. Blessed be the Spirit who wills to flow forth, true to that promise, through the being of even us.

(2) John 20:21-23. We step here into a very different scene. The stir and festal triumph of the Tabernacle Day are hushed. It is the glorious calm of the evening of the first Easter, in that large Upper Room, so carefully barred and bolted, where the disciples with gladness saw the Lord. I need not recite at length his blessed words, the very first words addressed to them *as a company* by him who now stood there amongst them in 'the power of an endless life' (Heb. 7:16). Enough to remember that they were words first of divine peace to themselves and then, immediately, words of mission, mission into the world, with a view to the 'remitting' and 'retaining' of sins. And this mission was accompanied by a marked and deeply significant action: 'he breathed on them, and saith unto them, Receive ye the Holy Ghost.'

Here again we might turn aside to more than one enquiry by the way; for example, to the question whether the Risen Lord's action of breathing was the sacrament, so to speak, of an immediate, or of a coming, gift of the Spirit; whether he then and there conveyed to them a special afflatus, or significantly assured them of the great afflatus so soon to come. But for our present purpose this enquiry is not necessary. In either case we gather unmistakably from the words and action some great spiritual facts. We see that the mission was one for which a special gift of the Spirit's power and presence was required. And we see that that gift was to be given in the very closest connection with the person and work of the Lord Jesus slain and risen again. The symbolic Breath came from his holy lips. As on the Pentecostal day, so now it was 'HE who shed forth', whether it was in act or in prospect, the Spirit, his Spirit, the Spirit of Christ, the Comforter in his blessed power, one with Christ, glorifying and imparting Christ.

As regards the terms of the mission I do not speak at length. Illustrated by the recorded work of the apostles and other first preachers of the gospel, it is surely plain what they do *not* mean. They do not mean that the divine pardon of the soul is so put in charge of any man, or any body of men, as that for one moment that man, or that body, even if the body were the whole church, can intercept the soul's direct appeal to the Lord and his direct voice of peace to the soul; or can provide a substitute for either. If this were the place, it would be easy to show how the claims of the Roman Catholic priesthood (and all really kindred claims) to act as intermediaries in the actual conveyance of divine remission are quite without ground either in Scripture or in really primeval antiquity after it; and how the application of the words of this passage to the work of the Christian presbyter comes up not till comparatively late in church history; and how even when the words were first so applied, the reference was understood to be to what we may call the church's pardon rather than the Lord's, to the ministry of exclusion from and re-admission to the ordinances and fellowship of the Christian community. But it may be enough now to say that Scripture itself abundantly witnesses to the apostles' own unconsciousness of the possession of a really mediatorial power and position; as for instance in the words of Peter to Simon Magus at Samaria (Acts 8:22). And the practically one alternative interpretation here is that the remission and retention are declaratory. The messengers here commissioned are to make known, for the world's need, how sin is forgiven in Christ, and how it is not forgiven.

And we surely gather that this work for the Lord is the work not of apostles only, not of the sacred ministry only, distinct and special as its functions are, but of the whole true church of Christ. More persons were present in the Upper Room than the apostles. Certainly the two friends from Emmaus were there, and those two had found on their arrival 'others with' the Eleven (Luke 24:33). And the Lord is at no pains to draw distinctions on this occasion, as he had been on others. No, he was empowering his whole true church, there present by representation before him, to be his delegate, his representative, in that part of his own mission from the Father which consisted in the unveiling to human hearts how sin is to be forgiven, how man is to enter into peace with God.

So here is a passage in which every true child of God, every true member of Christ our Head, may read what is to be the essence of his own life-work for him. It means no ecclesiastical anarchy, I am sure. The Lord is the God of order, not confusion (see 1 Cor. 14:33). But it does mean that there is no true order which would debar the humblest Christian from his part, or her part, in this most blessed 'work of service' (Eph. 4:12), this earnest, loving, 'holding out of the word of life' (Phil. 2:16). And on the other hand it solemnly, tenderly, reminds all such, as with the voice of Jesus himself, that the inmost qualification for that work is not mere energy of character, or ease of utterance, fancied fulness of knowledge, or even truth of view. It is the inbreathed and inbreathing presence of the Holy Spirit. If the message is to be not only true but truly carried, truthfully handled, presented as the solemn, blissful reality it is, the messenger, be he who he may, must be *spiritual*, must possess, must be possessed by, the Spirit of the Son of God. The Holy Ghost must have taught *him* indeed the realities of sin, and of its remission. The Holy Ghost must work in and through him as in a vessel meet for the Master's use. If he bears the commission and orders of the church of God let him thank his Master for the blessed privilege and advantage; but let him not forget that the church gave him that gift *on the solemn understanding* that he believed himself to be already in a special sense dealt with for the purpose by the Holy Ghost. And let the lay worker for the Lord equally remember that his title to be a witness-bearer of the way of salvation is vitally connected, as between him and his Saviour, with his being indeed spiritual, 'worshipping by the Spirit of God' (Phil. 3:3), 'walking by the Spirit' bringing forth the Spirit's holy, humble 'fruit' (Gal. 5:22, 25). So we come round again, in essence, though under quite different imagery, to the truth conveyed by John 7:38.

(3) 1 John 2:20, 27; 3:24. A very few words will suffice on these two passages of the precious First Epistle.

The former has been already treated incidentally, and little more needs saying here in this 'chapter of fragments' than to call the reader to observe the imagery of 'anointing' used by the apostle. The 'little child' in Christ is reminded by this that the gift to him of the illuminating Spirit, who pours through conscience, mind and affections the pure light of the eternal principles and truths of grace, constitutes him in his new life a 'king and priest' to his Father, and, in a humble but real sense, a 'prophet' too; a man who has, under the guidance of the Word of God, more than nature's insight into truth and error concerning salvation.

The second passage, with its truly heavenly context, will indeed reward close and prayerful study as the believing reader ponders the tender, gracious commandment (not commandments) to 'believe on the name of his Son, and to love one another'; the love being the sure outcome of the faith, just as far as the faith is true and full.

All that shall be said here is, of course, on the explicit reference to the blessed Spirit. What is its assertion? It is that the sure way to ascertain that God 'abideth in us' is, to render the Greek literally, 'out of the Spirit which he gave us'. From that blessed Gift our proofs must be drawn. And how and where shall we find them? The immediate following context gives part of the answer; it is by finding our souls respond with a full Amen to the scriptural revelation of the glory of the incarnate Son and his precious work. And the whole New Testament suggests the rest of the answer; it is by finding our wills respond with a love and loyalty which only God can give to his own description of 'the fruit of the Spirit', 'his will, even our sanctification', his holy humbling, chastening will.

(4) A few words on the manifested glory and work of the Holy Spirit as seen in the Book of Revelation shall close this chapter. The book abounds in mentions of him. They range from 1:4 – where beyond all reasonable question the reverent Bible student will see him, one but sevenfold, in those seven Spirits before the throne who are named *with and between* the Father and the Son as the source of grace and peace – to 22:17, where the Spirit with the Bride, the blessed life-giver with and through the Body which he fills with the true life, says 'Come' to the thirsty soul of man asking for the living water which is given in the gift of himself.

I have touched already, and perhaps sufficiently, on the beautiful phenomenon of Revelation 2, 3, the identification, or rather union, of the voice of Christ with the voice of the Spirit. It may be enough further to call attention to that one glorious passage where the exalted Redeemer, recent from the wounds of the cross, is seen 'having seven horns and seven eyes, which are the seven Spirits of God, sent forth into all the earth' (Rev. 5:6; see 3:1). The imagery, sublime in its boldness, carries manifestly with it some great truths concerning the relation of the Holy Spirit to the Lord Jesus and to his presence with his church below. It reminds us with peculiar and vivid force of the depth and closeness of the connection of life and work between the Spirit and the Son. It shows us, 'in the visions of God', how the Spirit is inherent in the Son, if I may dare say so, inherent with an unspeakable union of being, and harmony of will, and order of working;

and how he is sent forth by him, radiates forth from him. In particular it indicates that the glorified Christ, in all the exercises of his perfect power (the 'seven horns') and most real presence (the 'seven eyes') 'in all the earth', in all his dealings with and for his people here below, has, for the divine vehicle of that power and presence, the Holy Ghost in his sevenfold perfectness of gift and working. The effluent presence of the Lamb, if I may use the phrase, is made, is conveyed, for us on earth, for all the members 'in all the earth', by the Holy Ghost. It is he who in perfectness of power 'strengthens us in the inner man' that Christ in perfectness of presence may 'dwell in our hearts by faith' (Eph. 3:16, 17). It is by him that we are 'joined unto the Lord' (1 Cor. 6:17). It is he who makes the 'one body' (Eph. 4:4), by the union of each believer with the Head, and so with all the members. The force, the presence, the voice, of the Lord Christ Jesus – all is by the Spirit; not by physical, or quasi-physical, contact with the glorified Body of the Redeemer, but by part and lot in his Spirit.

'Where that Spirit is,' said the Dean of Llandaff a few years ago in the Cambridge University pulpit, 'there is the Body of Christ; and only there.'

Come then, blessed Spirit, evermore come, and in all the sevenfold fulness of thy infinitely gracious operation bring us the members into in every deeper union, spiritual, heavenly, holy, with him who is our Head.

Chapter 9

General View of Paul's Teaching

We approach the revelation of the blessed Comforter and his work given to us through Paul. In the present chapter we shall attempt a sort of general view of the subject, and in the remaining chapters seek to take up in more detail some of the greater and more commanding truths thus given.

It is a large and wonderful field. The writings of John, as we have seen, present us with a mass of treasure for our doctrine of the Spirit. On the great subject of his personality in particular their witness is supreme in importance. But the Epistles of Paul fairly overflow with the glorious theme of the Spirit and his work, and in respect of some of his redeeming and sanctifying operations their witness is practically unique. Is not this remarkable, let me ask by the way, this fulness of the doctrine of the Spirit *in Paul*? We are accustomed, and rightly, to regard Paul as the great commissioned teacher and vindicator of that other region of vital truth – our acceptance, our justification, for the Redeemer's merits, by faith in his blood, by simplest acceptance of the divine imputed righteousness. It is then all the more impressive to find that to this same Paul we must go for the fullest scriptural account of 'Christ in us' by the Spirit as well as of 'Christ for us' in his merits. If the precious sentences, 'Justified freely by his grace, through the redemption that is in Christ Jesus'; 'That he might be just and the justifier of him that believeth in Jesus'

(Rom. 3:24, 26), are deeply and distinctively Pauline, so too are those others: 'Your body is the temple of the Holy Ghost which is in you' (1 Cor. 6:19); 'the love of God is shed abroad in our hearts by the Holy Ghost' (Rom. 5:5); 'Strengthened with might by his Spirit ... that Christ may dwell in your hearts by faith' (Eph. 3:16, 17); 'Be ye filled with the Spirit' (Eph. 5:18); 'Walk by the Spirit' (Gal. 5:25); 'By the Spirit mortify the deeds of the body' (Rom. 8:13); and so on, through a long chain of utterances living and glowing with the blessedness of our divine life, and peace, and strength, and 'joy in the Holy Ghost' (Rom. 14:17).

In this double phenomenon of the writings of Paul – this large and jealous vindication on the one hand of the way of our acceptance through 'the obedience of the One' (Rom. 5:19) and through it alone, and yet this even more pervading and continuous assertion of our life and walk by the Spirit on the other hand – I read great and pregnant lessons. For one thing I learn that what God has so joined together man must not from either side put asunder, in faith, or teaching, or life. Perfectly distinct in conception, the two ranges of truth are indissolubly wedded together in purpose and in result. And for another thing I learn that in some all-important respects the one of these ranges of truth exists and is revealed for the sake of the other, and not the other for the sake of the one. Justification, acceptance, peace with God, redemption from the curse of the law – these things are revealed (thanks be to God, they are revealed) not for themselves, so to speak, as if they were ends and goals in the way of grace, but for the sake of our living by the Spirit, and walking by the Spirit, and being the living temples of the Spirit, and thus being conformed to the image of the Son of the Father, and entering thus on a never-ending course of 'serving in the newness of the Spirit' (Rom. 7:6).

Paul's writings, alike in their argument and in their proportions, are inspired reminders to us to keep these things related in our own thought, and faith, and life. We are redeemed from the just sentence of the broken law '*in order that* we may receive the promise of the Spirit by faith'; so it stands explicitly, and most memorably, in Galatians 3:13, 14. Not for one moment, really, are we viewed as simply saved from present and future wrath as if that were an end in itself, the change in our hearts and lives coming in merely as evidence that we are secure. That change is, we may boldly say, the absolutely necessary *raison d'être* of the work of ransom and acceptance. We are accepted that we may be holy; that we may live entirely to the Lord; 'that Christ may be magnified in our body' (Phil. 1:20); in other words that the blessed Spirit, now as it were liberated to flow upon us and to spring up within us, may have his way and will in all we are and all we shall be for ever.

Is it not so? And shall not our faith, our witness, our teaching, take this apostolic line? Shall we not stand fast, faster than ever, in the truth of the justifying righteousness received by faith alone, but so as always to enjoy and to commend the always related and always crowning truth of 'the promise of the Spirit', received also by faith alone? Happy the soul which, standing on the rock of the one truth drinks the inexhaustible fountain of the other, day by day, and hour by hour. Happy the church where that rock and that fountain alike 'do follow them', in the work of witness in word and in life to the reality of God in Christ.

So Christ shall be our daily food,
Our daily drink his precious blood ;
And thus the Spirit's calm excess
Shall fill our souls with holiness.

But it is time to come to some more detailed view of what Paul was guided to say of the glory and work of the Holy Ghost, and of the believer's dependence on him and power in him. Our view will not profess, however, to be at all exhaustive; the reader will find abundant gleanings left in the blessed field.

(1) The witness of Paul to the *personality* of the Spirit, though less full than that of the Lord Jesus in John, is unmistakable to the submissive reader. Nowhere indeed in Paul (in the Greek, though here and there in our Authorized Version) do we find masculine pronouns, he, him, his, used by the Spirit (e.g. Rom. 8:27; 1 Cor. 12:11). But we find in Paul that the Spirit can be not only 'quenched' but 'grieved' (1 Thess. 5:19; Eph. 4:30); that the Spirit 'intercedeth for the saints with unutterable groanings', and that 'he who searcheth the hearts' (Rom. 8:26, 27; see verse 6 in the Greek), regards the Spirit, in that intercession, as the bearer, the subject, of a 'mind', an intention, a characterizing thought. All this speaks of personality. And we find the Spirit revealed, through Paul, as the Lord of the 'temple' of the Christian's body (1 Cor. 6:19), and that in a context, which is as remote as possible from associations of mere poetry or figure. A person, and a divine person, is presented to us here as dwelling in us.

(2) The unspeakably deep *union of being and work between the Spirit and the Son* comes out clearly in Paul.

The Spirit is 'the Spirit of Christ' (Rom. 8:9); and in the immediate context there we see the two blessed persons so united that what in one breath is called the indwelling of the Spirit (Rom. 8:9) is called in the next the indwelling of Christ (Rom. 8:10), and this again the indwelling of the Spirit.

(3) When we come to the Pauline revelation of the *process of the work of grace* we find that from first to last, from the new birth to the coming glory, the Holy Spirit is the immediate agent, life-giving, life-sustaining. The true child of God is 'born after the Spirit' (Gal. 4:29). He 'lives *by* the Spirit' (Gal. 5:25; so render). It is the Spirit who unites him to his Lord, his vital Head; for 'he that is joined' in the mystic bridal 'to the Lord is one Spirit' (1 Cor. 6:17). It is the Spirit who in his own infinitely wise and effectual way makes known to him the reality and the sweetness of the eternal things so as he could not possibly know them by the powers of nature; for

> 'it is written, Eye hath not seen, nor ear heard, neither have entered into the heart of man the things which God hath prepared for them that love him; but God hath revealed them unto us by his Spirit.... We have received... the Spirit which is of God, that we might know the things which are freely given to us ($\tau\alpha$ $\chi\alpha\rho\iota\sigma\theta\epsilon\nu\tau\alpha$) of God.... But the natural man receiveth not the things of the Spirit of God; for they are foolishness unto him, neither can he know them, because they are spiritually discerned' (1 Cor. 2:9-14).

And his unveiling has to do, let us observe, not only with an eternal future but still more with a supernatural present. The main reference is to the present gifts of grace, the present and actual 'riches of Christ', which are ours, now

and here, in him. 'The things which eye hath not seen' are
not only, as we read it in one of the loveliest and most
pathetic of all English poems, the things 'beyond the clouds
and beyond the tomb'. They are the things which '*are,
have been,* freely given to us of God'. They are, in Peter's
magnificent words, 'all things which pertain to life and
godliness' (2 Pet. 1:3), and which now, as a fact, 'his divine
power *hath given us.*' They are a present fulness of divine
acceptance, and a present fulness of divine spiritual riches;

> 'Our never-failing treasury, fill'd
>   With boundless stores of grace.'

And so the Holy Spirit's work is to show us what we *at
this moment possess,* for our present wonder, and joy, and
use, and our present glorification of the Giver.

This interior revealing work of the indwelling teacher,
who is creator too, is set forth in detail in several passages
of Paul. Thus we see him, we hear him, imparting to us a
supernatural insight into our blessed new childhood, new
sonship, in the life and family of grace, and a supernatural
consciousness and assurance of it. 'Ye have received the
Spirit of adoption, whereby we cry, Abba, Father' (Rom.
8:15); 'God hath sent the Spirit of his Son into your hearts
crying Abba, Father' (Gal. 4:6); 'The Spirit itself beareth
witness with our spirit that we are the children of God and
if children then heirs' (Rom. 8:16, 17). In some way of his
own (let us leave the details of the holy secret to him), he
takes and teaches the believing sinner, and shows him the
strong, sweet, heavenly certainties of the Word of God *as
true for him,* so as not the most exact nor the most profound
exegesis without him could show them. Under his

mysterious touch of truth and love it becomes strangely and gladly clear that the promises and welcomes of grace mean what they say; that 'he that cometh' is 'in no wise cast out' (John 6:37), and that this 'not cast out' means a most glorious and wonderful 'welcomed in'; a union, a filiation, an incorporation into the blessed family of God, in the divine firstborn Brother, which implies beyond a doubt for the believing sinner all the adoptive privileges of sonship, and the full admission of the heavenborn child to the responsive intimacies of divine love.

The same view of the Spirit's work, though under less definite imagery, comes out in Romans 5:5: 'The love of God hath been poured out' (so literally) 'in our hearts by the Holy Ghost which is given unto us.' This has been explained by some to mean that he has now imparted to us, in rich effusion, a divine power *or faculty of loving;* has caused us to love with a love which is the love of God. I cannot but differ from such an exposition. With what it probably means at its heart, so to speak, I am entirely at accord. Fully assured I am that, while we can only love God with the same constitutional human faculty or moral organ, with which we love man, still our union by the Spirit with the blessed Head of regenerate manhood has put such a new condition into that organ, and connected it so with his love who is our life, that we may speak of our regenerate souls as loving with his love; *'in the heart of Jesus Christ',* as Paul expresses it (Phil. 1.8). With inmost assent of mind and faith would I echo these words of Miss Frances Havergal's:

'Thy love, thy joy, thy peace,
    Continuously impart

   Unto my heart,
Fresh springs that never cease
But still increase.'

Only I would use them as remembering always that this
most blessed connection and infusion never invades our
personality, nor annuls our responsibility.[1] But the context
of Romans 5 goes clearly, as it seems to me, against our
explaining 'the love of God' here of our love to him. It is
'his love which he commendeth toward us, in that, while
we were yet sinners, Christ died for us' (Rom. 5:8); a love
altogether his, not in origin only but in expression and
direction, while yet the manifestation of it to and in the
heart of the justified believer has everything to do with
his waking up to 'love the Lord his God with all' that
'heart'. And it is this manifestation which the blessed Spirit
effects; so we read here. Dwelling in the man he has

---

1. On this subject of our derivation of the whole secret of the
new life from our Head by the Spirit, see Walter Marshall, *Gospel
Mystery of Sanctification*. See particularly Direction iii., near the
beginning: 'One great mystery is that the holy frame and
disposition whereby our souls are furnished and enabled for
immediate practice of the law must "be obtained by receiving it
out of Christ's fulness", as a thing already prepared and brought
to an existence for us in Christ, and treasured up in him; and
that as we are justified by a righteousness wrought out in Christ
and imputed to us, so we are sanctified by such a holy frame
and qualifications as are first wrought out and completed in Christ
for us, and then imparted to us; ... so that we are not at all to
work together with Christ in making or producing that holy frame
in us, but only to take it to ourselves, and use it in our holy
practice, as made ready to our hands.' The whole context, and
indeed the whole book, are the best vindication of this statement,
which, in Marshall's sense of it, means to recommend anything
rather than a life of spiritual indolence.

regenerated, he so deals with the regenerate consciousness that the apprehension of mercy, the acceptance of acquittal, comes to be transfigured into an intuition into an 'everlasting love' as tender as it is almighty. The man finds, he knows not how, outpoured in his heart ($\dot{\epsilon}\kappa\kappa\dot{\epsilon}\chi\nu\tau\alpha\iota$), that 'rest is bliss', that 'sweet, pleasant, and unspeakable comfort', which rises direct from the certainty not that he loves but that he is thus wonderfully loved.

> 'Loved with everlasting love,
> Led by grace that love to know –
> Spirit, breathing from above,
> Thou has taught me it is so!'

We have here then a work of the Spirit of love, *supremely characteristic*. We shall see the presentation of it in yet more developed, vivid, and, as it were, concrete forms when we come in a later chapter to study Paul's later written words about the dwelling of Christ in the heart by faith (Eph. 3:17). And we find it, as we have already noticed, re-appearing in this same Roman Epistle, where 'the Spirit itself beareth witness with our Spirit that we are the children of God' (Rom. 8:16). Observe the phraseology there. The Spirit appears as witnessing not *to*, but *with*, our spirit; a statement of the precious facts which gives us a view of them not so clearly given in 5:5; for here, in 8:16, we have 'our spirit' brought in as a concurrent witness. On the Holy Spirit's part the 'witness' is, 'Doubtless thou art his child'; on our spirit's part the 'witness' is, 'Doubtless thou art my Father', seen, welcomed, chosen, loved as such by even me. And the two distinct lines of witness meet in one strong, happy, humble certainty.

The man thus dealt with by the Holy One is seen, in
Paul, as the subject of his presence and power in many a
sacred detail. In his human spirit he has so received the
Spirit that he is said, wonderful as the phrase is, to have
'the mind (φρονημα) of the Spirit', his moral characteristics. Our version of Romans 8:6, 'To be *spiritually-
minded* is life and peace', is inadequate while true. It fails
to give, as the literal version does, the truth of the unspeakable connection in the life of grace between the Spirit and
the spiritual man; the glorious mystery of the vital union
as it regards the Spirit's indwelling presence and power.
Reading literally, '*The mind of the Spirit* is life and peace'
(see verse 27), we see the believer, mortal, sinful, the
ceaselessly needy recipient of 'mercy from first to last',
yet so wonderfully visited and inhabited by his regenerator,
his sanctifier, that along the lines of his own real will,
understanding, and affections, there runs the power of the
personal presence, yea, of the personal character, of the
Lord, the life-giver. The more the man humbly, and in
watchfulness and prayer, but with entire willingness and
simplicity, 'yields himself unto God' (Rom. 6:13) thus
present, the more shall he, intact in personality, have
carried out in him the workings of that 'mind'.

And what will the result be? No sensationalism, no
fanaticism. A great conquest and captivity will be one side
of the result; 'every thought brought into captivity unto
the obedience of Christ' (2 Cor. 10:5).

A holy prayerfulness, deep and yearning, will be another
side of the result (Rom. 8:26; see Eph. 6:18, and Jude 20).

A loving, joyful, peaceful, trustworthy, meek, self-
controlled walk in human life and intercourse, will be
another (Gal. 5:22, 23).

A tendency towards all such union with other children of God as is obstructed by the life and spirit of self, will be another (1 Cor. 12:4; Eph. 2:18; 4:3, 4; Phil. 1:27; 2:1).

A joy and delight in adoration, and generally in being at the will and service of the adored Lord, will be another (Phil. 3:3).

A deepening consciousness of the truth, and conquering power of the Word of God, as the sword in the spiritual combat, will be another (Eph. 6:17).

A growing gladness in the experience of a meek and lowly but most real sacrifice and surrender in all things to God, will be another; as the believer realizes his union, by the Spirit, with him who 'by means of the eternal Spirit offered himself without spot to God' (Heb. 9:14).

A quiet readiness, as one aspect of the same blessed fact, to be 'led by the Spirit' (Rom. 8:14), will be another; and that leading will always be *out* of the way and will of self *into* that of God; out of the ambitions and interests of self into a daily aim and inmost choice and longing that 'Christ may be magnified in my body' (Phil. 1:20), that I may 'shew forth the praises of him who hath called me out of darkness into his marvellous light' (1 Pet. 2:9), that I may be, for the help of all around me, 'a vessel meet for the Master's use' (2 Tim. 2:21), an implement ready to his hand.

And another side of the result of having 'the mind of the Spirit' will be a larger insight into what is meant by a life of faith, a life of unreserved reliance on the promise and will of God, a reliance ever more childlike in its simplicity and ever more mature, and strong and prevailing in its results. For the faith by which Christ dwells in the heart is but the effect in my soul and will of the blessed

Spirit's 'strengthening' (Eph. 3:16, 17). He is the 'Spirit of *faith*' (2 Cor. 4:13). And on the other hand it is 'by faith', by the simplest faith, that we 'receive the promise of the Spirit' (Gal. 3:14), as regards his developed inworking and empowering.

And if we take that aspect of the regenerate life which has specially to do with 'victory and triumph against the devil, the world, and the flesh', the three-fold ever-present enemy, how great are the assurances given us in the writings of Paul, as regards the power and working of the Holy Spirit! All Bible readers are familiar with the antitheses, so especially Pauline, between 'the flesh' and 'the Spirit'. But not all are familiar with the fact, which surely comes out under any careful enquiry, that by the Spirit, in such connections, the apostle habitually means not a 'better self' or 'nobler powers' of even regenerate man, but the indwelling Paraclete himself. So that the man who 'sows to the Spirit' (Gal. 6:8) means the man who casts the seed, so to speak, of all life's experiences upon that divine soil; in other words commits it to the Holy Ghost within him to deal victoriously with temptation and to put forth as the result of the fruit of holiness. And the man who in the realities of our life in the body, that body which is practically our one immediate vehicle of contact of all things with the world around, 'mortifies the machinations (πραξεις) of the body' (Rom. 8:13), does it, if he does it indeed 'by the Spirit'. He brings to bear upon the whole range of motion and solicitation to evil, incident to him as a dweller in 'this tabernacle', the glorious fact that 'he is joined unto the Lord, one Spirit'; that his 'body is the temple of the Holy Ghost, which he hath of God, and that he is not his own' (1 Cor. 6:17, 19).

He recalls Galatians 5:16, 17: 'Walk by the Spirit, and ye shall not fulfil the lust of the flesh; for the flesh lusteth (ἐπιθυμει) against the Spirit, and the Spirit against the flesh; and these are contrary the one to the other; so that ye cannot do the things that ye would.' Is not that passage too often read as if verse 17 had nothing to tell us but (what it assuredly *does* tell us) that the 'infection of nature doth remain, yea, in them that are regenerated', and that to the last? True; it is a truth of constant merciful humiliation and caution. But what is the main purpose of the apostle in this passage? Is it not emphatically to press the bright side on the antithesis, the side of peace, and victory, and liberty, and power? Its message, in the context, is altogether one of encouragement. It is written, like the treasures of truth in 1 John, 'in order that we may not sin' (1 John 2:1). Paul is intent on showing the believer how, although 'the flesh' is always present, carrying with it always the ingredients, so to speak, of the experience analysed in detail in Romans 7:17-24, there yet is something else always present also, and present in force. It is 'the Holy Ghost given unto us'. It is the living and personal Comforter, dwelling in our body, and making present in us 'the life of Jesus' (2 Cor. 4:10, 11). It is the Spirit 'lusting against the flesh' – a force, a tendency, a personal power, on the side of our deliverance and victory, gloriously competent to overcome its antagonist, and to make us, the subjects of it, as we yield to it and welcome it, mercifully, 'unable *to do the things we would'* in the life of the flesh, in the life of self.

So 'there is liberty where the Spirit of the Lord is' (2 Cor. 3:17); a blessed liberty, meek and lowly, but strong and thankful too. We find an emancipation from 'old sins'

(2 Pet. 1:9), and a wonderful precaution and prophylactic[2] against new ones, in the secret of the indwelling strength, or rather Strengthener, who is not ourselves yet is as near to us as ourselves. He is at the same time our always enlightening convincer, as he unfolds to us the divine holiness and our 'exceeding need'. But also, blessed be God, we shall find in him, as we welcome him, our internal liberator, present always, not sometimes only; our 'victory and triumph' in a way which forebodes no exhaustion by its own efforts, for it is the almighty One, working in us. We come very quickly, in the interior conflict, to the edge of our own strength. But, to rest upon the presence of 'the Spirit lusting against the flesh' is to repose upon a power which has no edge, and no bottom. And *conscious weakness* is that which reposes most simply and most effectually upon it.

Let me close this brief general view with the remark that no call is louder to the church, and to the Christian, of the present day than that we hasten to discover (if we still have that to do), and then always watchfully to use, our 'great strength' in the Spirit of God for deliverance from 'serving sin', that so we may be filled with his 'calm excess', and may overflow for blessing in the world around. The call, for one and for another, may not be to a life of any extraordinary apparent sacrifice, or external exhaustion or hardship; though who may say that it shall not be so? But most assuredly, for all who would be on the Lord's side in these days of ours, it is a call to a life of just such 'coming out and being separate' from the world externally (while yet we are ready every hour lovingly to serve that world for our Lord) as arises from a true

---

2. prophylactic – preventative against disease.

separation from the life of self and of sinning internally. How shall it be? How shall we indeed be sanctified, sinners that we are, in order to this witness and service of word and work? There is only one way. It is 'in the name of the Lord Jesus, and by *the Spirit* of our God' (1 Cor. 6:11).

Chapter 10

The Fruit of the Spirit

A general view of the revelation through Paul of the Holy Spirit and his work lies now before us. We proceed in the chapters which remain to a more detailed study of some leading Pauline passages, in which the Spirit's blessed operation and its results stand out manifested with peculiar glory. May our 'meditation of him', by his great grace, 'be sweet' (Ps. 104:34). May thought and word be in some true sense his, and may the whole result be for him.

I take up in the present chapter the great passage about the *fruit* of the Spirit, generated and produced in 'the spiritual man' (Gal. 5:22, 23). The words thus specially before us are part of a context, and indeed of an Epistle, full to overflow of the truth of the Holy Ghost. What we observed in the last chapter regarding the doctrine of Paul in general is seen in the Galatian Epistle, and in this section of it, eminently.

The Epistle is an urgent protest against a false doctrine of justification. It states with a strong and jealous firmness and precision the truth of the finished work of the atoning cross, and the absolute necessity and simplicity of the function of faith, faith only, in order to the sinner's entrance into the merits of the Crucified, into acceptance in him who 'brought us out from the curse, being made a curse for us' (Gal. 3:13). It protests that a gospel which leaves this out, which has not this for its message, is not a gospel but a fatal perversion of the gospel. But does the Epistle still stand there? Is justification its whole message? No; it conveys quite as much a warning, a testimony, an affirmation, about the work and power of the Holy Ghost. The all-importance, for Paul, of the truth of justification resides after all in this, and that for the justified, and for them only, lies open the life, and walk, and victory, and fruit-bearing, which is by the Holy Ghost alone. As guilty sinners they take refuge by faith in Jesus Christ 'made a curse for them'; and then, and so, they become possessed of all that is laid up in that same Saviour risen and glorified, and who now by the same Spirit who led them to him dwells in them.

So in this Epistle of justification, as it draws to its wonderful close, we have more and more of the Holy Ghost. 'Walk by the Spirit, and ye shall not fulfil the lust of the flesh' (Gal. 5:16); let us observe the definiteness and decision of that promise, my Christian brother and reader, and humbly claim it. Again, 'The flesh lusteth against the Spirit, and' (we dwelt on this divine side of the matter in the last chapter) 'the Spirit against the flesh.'

Again, 'If ye be led by the Spirit, ye are not under the law' (Gal. 5:17, 18); not in collision with it, as it is the royal proclamation of your Father's will. Do you challenge his inspection as solely and only *Judge*? Ah, that would to the last involve a sternly judicial condemnation. But do you lovingly, and with the heart of the child born again of the Spirit, look up to him as *Father*, and, giving yourself to be led along the way of his will by his Spirit, say, 'Oh how I' (not challenge, but) 'love thy law' (Ps. 119:97), thy will revealed? Then indeed, as regards your personal relation to that law, you are not 'under it'; it is not 'over you' as the judicial sword. Not only has your blessed redeemer met it for you as you have violated it, and as you fall short of it; you also now, in a sense most humble, led by the Spirit, meet it with the sincerity of a loyal will, loving the Law-giver 'from the soul' (Eph. 6:6; so literally).

Again, a few verses later, comes the significant precept, 'If we live by the Spirit', if indeed we have by his power the new birth and life, 'let us also *take step by step* (στοιχωμεν) *by the Spirit'*. Let us consciously, with recollection, and *in detail,* apply our life-power, yield to our life-giver, in the daily path. Not only as to the large scope of existence but in the minutest things of this hour, in the small but strong temptations of ordinary intercourse, in the facile commonplace occasions for loss of temper, loss of humility, loss of purity, failure to love, to serve, to remember that we are not on our own, let us 'take step by step' by the Holy Ghost. Can I too earnestly press that precept, with all its speciality of phrase in the Greek, upon my reader, upon myself?

Again, a little further on we have 'the Spirit of *meekness'* (Gal. 6:1); the blessed Paraclete ready to guide us 'step by step' through one of the specially rough and crooked places of common Christian life.

And a little lower again, in a passage which we have touched upon in the last chapter, we find the Christian entreated to 'sow to the Spirit' (Gal. 6:8), to cast, by faith, upon the presence and power of the Holy Ghost within him as upon a divine soil, the seed given by each trying incident of life. The issue of such sowing shall be 'life everlasting'; developments of the life of God within him now, and eternal developments from each such sowing hereafter, to his glory.

But I must not pursue too far, though it is all to the purpose, the context of our special passage, nor the general teaching of this Epistle on the relations between acceptance in Christ and life by the Holy Ghost. We come now at once to a view of the fruit of the Spirit.

Here we first observe the light thrown by contrast on the word 'fruit'. Just before we have had recounted to us 'the *works* of the flesh' (Gal. 5:19-21). The difference of the phrases is significant. In the one the noun in question is plural, in the other singular. A weary course of discords and internal collisions, a life in pieces and out of joint, is thus contrasted with a life whose growth is one harmonious development from one rich central principle, germinating and *fructifying* into a result of purity and peace. Here is already a lesson for the spiritual man. As far as the Holy Spirit is in possession of him, as far as he is being led by the Spirit, and is yielding himself to the will and mind ($\phi\rho\acute{o}\nu\eta\mu\alpha$) of the Spirit, so far is his life set free from the internal wear and restlessness of 'the works of the flesh' (Rom. 8:6), and drawn together into a peace and unity which is possible only where what is made for God rests in him and lives for him.

But this singular number, this 'fruit', not 'fruits', of the passage before us, has more to say, besides this lesson of contrast. It reminds the Christian, as he reads over the blessed list of elements in the heavenly fruit, that they are essentially parts of one thing, and not isolated things, in the Lord's idea of the servant's life. They are not separable characters, but a character. They are not put before the man who 'lives by the Spirit' in order that he may pick and choose, and prefer to develop some one or two of them, perhaps those which he feels instinctively have most

affinity with his natural dispositions. They are in the divine
intention always inter-related, indivisible; the whole
character of the Christian. We may compare the Beatitudes
(Matt. 5:3-12), which assuredly describe not various
persons but one person, the true disciple of Jesus Christ
seen from many points of view. And we may compare
also that remarkable passage, 2 Peter 1:5-7, where, under
widely different phraseology, the believer, the man who
has 'obtained precious faith', is entreated to 'give all
diligence' to seek for a holy completeness and harmony
in the manifestation through him of the life of God which
is in him.

That passage, by the way, may caution us against a
disproportionate inference from the precious imagery of
'the fruit' in this. The ideas suggested by fruit and
fruitbearing are not those of effort and care in the
fruitbearing branch; effort and care are the cultivator's part.
But Peter reminds us that the analogy between the
impersonal fruit-tree and the personal believer cannot be
in all respects complete. In the conscious and responsible
man, as such, there must always be place for 'all diligence'.
Such 'diligence' does not create life, or generate it, nor
does it in a direct way develop the issues of life. But
diligence is the believer's duty in connection with that
development; it means, if done in spirit and in truth, the
believer's 'laying aside' (1 Pet. 2:1) in the Lord's name
every known thing that *hinders* the outgrowth and fulness
of the fruit.

But, when this is said, by way of balance and clear-
ness, then without reserve we can throw our thankful attention upon the blessed suggestions and significance of
the word 'fruit'. What does it tell us? It tells us, the

branches of the true Vine, that in us, yet not of us, there is
a mighty fructifying *principle*. It tells us that the holy characteristics, the holy character, here painted before us must
not be worked up by weary efforts out of the materials of
self, somewhat re-adjusted and assisting one another's
weakness, if they could do so. The happy, pure phenomenon has a nobly adequate vital *cause* behind it. It grows;
it is not manufactured. It is not acquired from our surroundings, but produced amidst them. It is the result of a
secret of life; life, that most wonderful of forces, while
most silent; the force which in the natural world can, in
the tender shoots of the young tree, lift the massive stone,
and rend the joints of rock-like masonry; and which in the
spiritual world can make the weak strong, and do silent
miracles with what once seemed impossibilities in character within and circumstances without.

Let the anxious, the discouraged, Christian ponder this
word 'fruit', recollecting this its special significance. Let
it remind him where his 'great strength' lies. It lies in
nothing that is properly and personally his. All that is his,
all such that is not sin, is capable indeed of wonderful use
by his 'great strength'. Gifts, talents, faculties of mind, or
body, or estate, be they very large or very, very small, all
are precious, all are usable. But none, absolutely none, is
his true strength. That lies wholly in a divinely given secret,
principle, force, which is in him but not of him, and whose
power is not for a moment to be measured by his weakness.
'From it is his fruit found' (see Hos. 14:8). Let him be at
rest about the adequacy of that cause to produce the effect
of holiness. Let him in humble faith 'lay aside' all known
hindrance; and then in the same humble faith, watching
and praying, but not struggling to force out the mighty

life, let him 'yield himself unto God' (Rom. 6:13) for a divinely natural fruitfulness.

For this fruit is 'the fruit of *the Spirit*'. Here is the all-important and all-welcome fact for us, in our present enquiry. This vital secret, force, principle, of which we have spoken – what is it? No abstract truth, no ideal of duty, no awe-inspiring but never life-giving '*I ought*'. It is the Holy Ghost, the personal and loving Paraclete. It is the Lord, the life-giver, whose tender and mighty working has drawn me to Christ, and knit me into him, and imparted him to me, blessed be his Name. Because of him, by virtue of him, thanks to him, through him indwelling, inworking, filling, welcomed in to have his way in his temple, the fruit of holiness begins to be, to grow, to come forth, to take its gracious shape, to ripen into its sweetness for the service of God and man (1 Cor. 6:19). And so our way, our indirect way, to contribute to the blessed result is clear. It is to remove in his name, the obstacles, but then to remember with thankful and peaceful joy that the work of life and fruit-producing, is his alone. *From this point of view,* my part is a blessed and wakeful Quietism;[1] a rest that he may work.

Need I at any length remind my reader that this view of the operation of *the Spirit* as the secret of the fruit of holiness leaves wholly inviolate the primary truth that '*Christ* is our life'? We saw early in our enquiry how clear and full is the certainty of that truth (Col. 3:4); that while the Spirit of God is the life-giver, the Son of God is the life. But then, the Spirit *is* the life-giver. By him, in his

---

1. I use the word Quietism to express *one side of truth,* and only so. In the history of theological language it has some associations with dangerous error.

infinitely gracious personal operation, you and I 'have the Son' (1 John 5:12). And his own divine, vital connection with the Son is such that where he is, savingly, there Christ is, and where Christ is, there he is. If I may quote words of my own written elsewhere: 'The Spirit is the eternal and divine personal vehicle; Jesus Christ, "who is our life", is the thing conveyed.... To borrow an imperfect analogy from physical science, Christ is as the sun of the soul, the Spirit is as the luminiferous ether by whose vibration we have the sun's light and heat.'

And now we come to Paul's delineation of this pure and sweet fruit of the Spirit. Let us take it up for a few very practical enquiries and remarks.

The first point for observation, an obvious one, but none the less to be definitely considered, is that the fruit of the Spirit consists in its essence not of doing but of being. There is nothing in this description which directly speaks of energetic enterprise, multiplied labours, severe sufferings, great material sacrifices. The activities of life are in fact almost absent from the immediate view, and the passive, the patient, aspect of the spiritual man's contact with life and men alone very visibly present.

What do we read in this? That the spiritual man is called, as his highest calling, to cut himself off from active, willing, practical service of others? That the celestial fruit will grow, and ripen, and be ready for the festival of God, most favourably in a 'life of contemplation', in a desert, or a cloister, or a jealously isolated study? The whole New Testament negatives such a thought. In it, the ideal Christian life is the life in which the Lord is glorified and manifested amidst the manifold relative duties and labours of the life of home, of citizenship, of public ministry, of active evangelization. It is a life in which the cross is daily carried, – the cross not of our wilful and ambitious choosing but of the Lord's humbling and searching allotment in the daily path. If the life of a monastery were contemplated in the New Testament at all, as it is not, surely it would be presented there as a 'counsel' not 'of perfection' but of imperfection; a lower path of surrender and of service, while the higher path was that of the mother, the child, the servant, who in the midst of common life 'did the will of God and soul' (Eph. 6:6).

But then, the impartial gospel does not say that work is therefore life. It points to the eternal necessity of right being in order to right doing. It bids the Christian live to serve, but live *behind his service* in and with his Lord and Life. It asks, ultimately, not whether to give your goods to the poor, or your body to the fire, but whether you love (1 Cor. 13:3).

So 'the fruit of the Spirit' is a divinely given and developed *character*, drawn out of the fulness of Christ; a character which must express itself in service, but whose essence 'is hid with Christ in God' (Col. 3:3). This is the 'fruit' which, according to the Lord Jesus Christ's own words, we shall surely bear if by the Spirit 'we abide in him' (John 15:4-8). Of this fruit, says the same teacher, we are to bear 'much', to the glory of his Father. We may or may not, in his providence, have much to do for him in enterprise, in effort, in public testimony, in memorable suffering. Perhaps his will for us, as we submit ourselves wholly to it, humbly ready to 'toil and not faint in his name, may be to do the most silent of domestic duties, or to bear the most exhausting weakness or pain in a neglected sick-room. But these questions touch the accidents of the

matter, not the essence. The 'fruit' is the character drawn
for us by the Holy Spirit from Jesus Christ our Head. The
'much fruit' is that character not stunted and dwarfed by
the frosts of unbelief, but expanding in sweet and strong
development in the sunny open air of the simplest faith.

And now we look at the particulars of the description,
at the elements which this inspired analysis shows us in
the texture of this fruit of Paradise grown on earth.

Those elements are nine: 'Love, joy, peace, long-
suffering, gentleness, goodness, faithfulness, meekness,
self-control.' And we may without over-refinement trace
a threefold grouping in the nine. 'Love, joy, peace', if I
read their reference aright, describe the character in its
immediate relation to the Lord, who is its spring of 'love',
its cause of 'joy', its living law of eternal 'peace'. 'Long-
suffering, gentleness, goodness' describe it in its relations
with men, as the Christian comes evermore from the 'secret
of the presence' to live his 'hidden' life, unharmed and
bearing blessing with it, amidst 'the plotting of men' and
'the strife of tongues' (Ps. 31:20). 'Faithfulness, meekness,
self-control' denote the Christian's characteristics not so
much under the trials of opposition or provocation as in
the common calls and duties of the day. And so the 'fruit'
appears in its fair roundness and ripeness.

So the man, born of the Spirit, led of the Spirit, is filled
with this same blessed Spirit (a 'filling' of which we shall
say more in the next chapter), lives, moves, and has his
being, with and for God and man. He is one personality,
and so his regenerate and Spirit-developed character is
one, from the 'love' to the 'self-control'; from his inmost
intercourse with his Lord to his act of most watchful and
practical self-discipline in open human life. What he is as

indeed a Christian, *in toto,* that is the Spirit's fruit.

As we close, let us observe some main truths about our Christian character, conveyed to us in this view of the fruit of the Spirit.

First, it is a character essentially of love and light. There are other qualifying facts about it assuredly. There is in the true Christian a gravity, an earnestness, a recollectedness, the lack of which would put the man out of character. This we have set before us here in the word 'temperance', self-control. But the material, the essence, of the life and character thus governed and controlled is 'love, joy, peace'. Let the disciple remember this, and see that nothing hinders the manifestation of it. He is a man in whom dwells that Spirit whose special function it is to 'pour out the *love* of God in the heart' (Rom. 5:5). That Spirit was shed upon the exalted Head as 'the oil of *gladness'* (Heb. 1:9), and as such he flows down upon the member of that Head to give him *'joy* in the Holy Ghost' (Rom. 14:17; see Phil. 3:3). And he is the Dove of divine *peace* (Rom. 8:6); his 'mind' is 'peace' as well as 'life'; he is 'the Spirit of faith' (2 Cor. 4:13), and 'peace' as well as 'joy' comes by 'believing' (Rom. 15:13). His unhindered inworking must come out then in a life which the known love of God makes *loving* – loving towards the Lord, and, in the Lord, towards men; *joyful,* with a calm but contagious and beneficent happiness, in its blessed certainty of Christ possessed in his glorious fulness; and *peaceful,* with a restfulness which cannot but diffuse itself around, as the Spirit shows our spirit that 'we have peace with God' (Rom. 5:1) and that the 'peace of God' can indeed 'keep our hearts and thoughts, in Christ Jesus' (Phil. 4:7). Let us remember, let us yield ourselves up, that we may manifest this essential threefold brightness of the life and character of the spiritual man. The Holy Ghost, giving us possession of Christ, is the heavenly antidote to coldness, to 'unpleasantness', to reserve of sympathies and service, to melancholy, to beclouding 'worry'. Self-control may have to carve deep lines in heart and life; but the chisel need never deface the brightness of the material.

Again, the character of the spiritual man is, in the relations of man with man, a character which is essentially ready to give way, to forbear, to bear. No elaborate qualification is needed here of this statement. I remember well what energy for service the Holy Spirit can and does impart to the weakest, and what immovable firmness for truth, for principle. He can, and does, develop in the most sensitive and timid. But deep below such manifestations, where they are indeed his work, there lies in the order of grace the presence, by his indwelling, of a tender and willing *surrender to others,* because first to the Lord, of every mere claim and jealousy of self. In proportion to the fulness of the Spirit's inworking, Jesus Christ really occupies the throne usurped before by self. And in proportion of that occupation of the throne by its true King, the man will be, more than anything else – whatever else he has to be in the direction of activity and firmness – 'long-suffering, gentle, good'.

Lastly, the truly spiritual character will, in its God-given development, issue always in a practical and wakeful life. Bright with a secret happiness, long-suffering with a deep and genuine surrender, the spiritual man will be 'faithful'[2]

---

2. That the word $\pi\iota\sigma\tau\iota\varsigma$ in this passage means 'faithfulness' not 'faith' is clear by its collocation with words in which relative duties are plainly in view. See, *e.g.,* Titus 2:10.

in every particular duty. He will be loyal to every promise made or trust undertaken. He will be to be depended upon in the business of the day. His correspondents will receive punctual answers; his friends, faithful and careful counsel. His employers will get a service out of him in which their best interests will be as his own. His servants and dependants will find him watchfully equitable, considerate, and courteous. He will take great care to 'owe no man anything' (Rom. 13:8). His church and parish will be truly served, be they ever so large, or small, or unresponsive. He will be known to be one who will take trouble for others, and who is glad to be their servant indeed for Jesus' sake. He will be *meek*, in the sense of a jealous avoidance of a manner and habit of self-assertion among his brethren in matters of opinion or of work.

And with and over it all he will be *self-controlled*. He will, for the glory of his Master, and that he may be truly serviceable among his fellows for him, watch and pray over his own acts and habits; over bed, board, and literature, and companionship, and recreation, and imagination, and tongue. Not that he will try to exercise the Stoic's fancied empire of self over self; but he will humbly, recollectedly, with decision, bring the whole of his life, hour by hour, to his glorious Master for orders and for discipline. He will 'keep under his body, and bring it into subjection' (1 Cor. 9:27), by a steadily maintained surrender of it as 'a living sacrifice' (Rom. 12:1) in all its faculties, to him of whom it is written, 'the body is for the Lord, and the Lord for the body' (1 Cor. 6:13). For the spiritual man, a true self-surrender is the deep secret of a true self-control.

So we shut the Epistle, and close our enquiry into the fruit of the Spirit. But we will do so only to turn again to life with a fuller recollection of what is the character we are intended to bear as spiritual men, and what is the divine provision, present and perfect, for the being of that character in us and its manifestation by us.

We will take the Scripture to be to us, amongst other things, a touchstone of our spiritual health. Not long ago I heard of a pious and devoted woman who used it habitually for this purpose. If in any degree conscious of a decline or obscuration in her life and work for her Lord, she took Galatians 5:22, 23, and read the words over as in his presence, and asked herself before him in what particular of the fruit of the Spirit any recent failure was apparent. Such asking and finding led at once to a repentant renewal of surrender and of faith, and so back to the rest, and to the readiness, which are for us, by the Holy Ghost, in Jesus Christ our Life.

Chapter 11

The Fulness of the Spirit

We are still engaged upon the revelation through Paul of
the Holy Spirit and his work. In the present chapter we
take up a group of Pauline words and phrases on the
subject, rich in materials for enquiry and for faith.

And, first, and mainly, the *fulness of the Spirit*. The
precise phrase is not Pauline; indeed it is not verbally
biblical. But equivalent expressions are abundant, in many
parts of Scripture. In the Mosaic age we find the sacred
artificer Bezaleel 'filled with the Spirit of God' (Exod.
31:3) for the work of constructing and adorning the
Tabernacle, whose true designer was none other than the
Holy Spirit (Heb. 9:8). In the gospel age the Lord Jesus
himself is seen going up from baptism to temptation 'full
of the Holy Ghost' (Luke 4:1). His forerunner was 'filled
with the Holy Ghost, even from his mother's womb'. And
both the father and mother of the second Elijah were on
special occasions 'filled with the Holy Ghost' (Luke 1:15,
67, 41). At Pentecost the gathered company, apparently
the 'hundred and twenty' of Acts 1:15, 'were all filled
with the Holy Ghost' (Acts 2:4). Peter was specially 'filled'
when he met the Jewish Council for the first time,
witnessing to his Lord (Acts 4:8, 31); and so, immediately
afterwards, were all the brethren. So was Paul at his
baptism (Acts 9:17), and when he sentenced Elymas to
blindness. So were the disciples at the Pisidian Antioch in

their hour of trial and joy (Acts 13:9, 52). The seven 'deacons' were chosen as 'men of honest report, full of the Holy Spirit and wisdom' (Acts 6:3). And Stephen, in the act of confession, 'being full of the Holy Ghost, saw heaven opened' (Acts 7:55). Barnabas is described as a man 'full of the Holy Ghost and of faith' (Acts 11:24).

Such are the main Scriptural parallels which by way of illustration may be gathered around the great Pauline passage on the fulness of the Spirit, Ephesians 5:18: 'Be not drunk with wine, wherein is excess, but *be ye filled in the Spirit.*'

Let us approach the text through the avenue of the parallels, and ask what they have to tell us on this great and precious fact and phenomenon of the new life.

Two kinds of filling

In the first place, we gather very plainly that 'the filling' is not identical in idea, whether or no it coincides in time, with the initial work of the Spirit as the life-giver. The filling is always seen as taking place where there is already present the new birth; and the possession of that birth is thus the occasion for a holy desire and longing to possess in some sense the filling.

Again we gather that there are, upon the whole, two main aspects or phases of the fulness of the Spirit. There is a special, critical phase, in which at a great crisis it comes out in marked, and perhaps wholly abnormal manifestation, as when it enables the man or woman to utter supernatural prediction or proclamation. And there is also what we may call the habitual phase, where it is used to describe the condition of this or that believer's life day by day and in its normal course. Thus the Seven

were not so much specially 'filled' as known to be 'full';
and so was Barnabas. Into this holy habitual fulness Paul
entered, it appears, at his baptism. On the other hand the
same Paul experienced from time to time the other and
abnormal sort of filling; and it thus results that the same
man might in one respect be full while in another he needed
to be filled.

There is a close connection from one point of view
between the fulness of the Spirit and what we commonly
mean by miraculous powers and works, particularly the
miraculous work of infallibly 'inspired' speaking. The
immediate result at Pentecost was an instantaneous
'speaking with other tongues, as the Spirit gave them
utterance' (Acts 2:4). Peter, Paul, Stephen, all spoke
supernatural words of testimony, or authority, or vision,
when thus 'filled with the Spirit'. The Lord Jesus himself
in the fulness of the Spirit sustained six weeks of fasting
and met the tempter under mysterious conditions. And
some may think that we should infer a similar reference
wherever the fulness is spoken of; as if it implied a miracle-
working power for instance in the Pisidian Christians, or
in the Ephesians who are here enjoined to be 'filled in the
Spirit'.

But it seems clear that this inference is by no means
necessary. And the proof of this statement lies in the
general testimony of the Word of God, which now in
successive chapters we have been collecting, to the
character of the *highest ranges* of the Holy One's work.
Those highest ranges have to do with not the miraculous,
in our common sense of that word, but the moral; the
transfiguration of the will, of the heart, of the soul, by the
immediate action of the Lord the Spirit. And there would

be surely an anomaly, a disproportion, in a real *appropriation* of the glorious phraseology of his fulness to the abnormal and (from a true viewpoint) not noblest and most perfect kind of his operation.

As we study the description of the fruit of the Spirit, and (what will be before us in our closing chapter) the indwelling of Christ in the heart by the Spirit, we are surely right in being certain that, whatever the fulness has to do with tongues and prophecies, it has its very highest concern with the believer's spiritual knowledge of his glorious Lord in the life of faith, and with the true manifestation of that life in the loveliness of a holy walk. To be filled with the Spirit is a phrase intensely connected with the fulness of our consecration to the will and work of God in human life.

The purpose of the miraculous

I would not be mistaken, as if I meant to relegate off-hand to the apostolic age alone all manifestations of the presence and power of God through his people in the way of sign and wonder. I do gather, both from the history of the church and from that pregnant Scripture, 1 Corinthians 13:8, that *on the whole* the commonly called miraculous displays of that power were intended for the first days only, or at least in a degree altogether peculiar. That period had characteristic conditions and needs which can never quite recur, even where the gospel is a new thing among the heathen of our time. For the gospel was then everywhere and absolutely new, with no history as yet behind it, no results of long years to give it their credentials.

I do not think, with some earnest Christians, that the Christian church is 'responsible' for the abeyance of

miraculous manifestation, by a lack of faith while faith
might at any time, claim the wonder-working power. I
believe on the other hand that subtle dangers and strong
temptations lie concealed where the Christian, or the
community, is eager for the gift of such miraculous
faculties rather than for an ever-deepening abasement of
self before the Holy One and an ever closer and more
chastened walk with him.

But meanwhile it is no part of such convictions to deny
à priori the possibilities of signs and wonders in any age,
our own or another, since the apostolic. Only it seems to
me to be certain not merely that *upon the whole* such
operation is not the will of God now as it was of old, but
that this is so because more and more his people are to be
led in his plan of teaching to rest in that 'more excellent
way' which already in that wonderful age the apostle
preferred to even 'the best gifts' (1 Cor. 12:31) of the other
kind.

But let us now take up the Apostle's word to the Ephesians:
Be ye filled with the Spirit; πληρουσθε ἐν Πνευματι.

It will be seen, as we look into the context, and as we
recall what has now been said on the two phases of
manifestation of the fulness, that we have here a precept
not for a crisis but for the whole habit of the Christian's
life. Not the least reference to works of wonder occurs in
the context. 'Psalms, and hymns, and spiritual songs', are
the manifestation of the fulness specially and at once in
view, and the blessed habit of thankfulness, and the
habitual readiness to forget self in the interests of others,
and then all the lovely details of the life of a sanctified
home. And we must observe that the perceptive verb

($\pi\lambda\eta\rho o\upsilon\sigma\theta\epsilon$) is in the present or continuing tense. It enjoins a course, a habit, not a critical effort or venture. It lays it upon the believer so to use the open spiritual secrets of his life in the Lord as to enter upon and walk in a state of divine fulness which shall be, above all things, useful and rich in blessing for the needs of the daily path, and shall result, whatever else it results in, in a temper of continual modesty and unselfish serviceableness towards all around him.

We must observe further the exact wording of the phrase in its last words: 'Be ye filled *in* the Spirit, $\dot{\epsilon}\nu\,\Pi\nu\epsilon\upsilon\mu\alpha\tau\iota$.' It is as if the apostle had written at large, 'Be filled *with* that Holy Spirit *in* whom you are; you *are in* the Spirit, if so be that the Spirit of God dwell in you' (Rom. 8:9); see now to it that by his grace you are in such relations of faith and submission with him that he who is within you shall be no longer, if hitherto, a well-head hidden beneath the *débris* of disobedience and unbelief, but springing, rising, unhindered in his blessed overflow, till *all* regions of the inner man "live" indeed where that "river cometh" (Ezek. 47:9); till *all* parts of your outward walk and work are ruled by the Spirit of God, and a holy abundance goes forth through you to the blessing of the souls of others' (John 7:38, 39).

Such, I believe is a simple account of the fulness of the Spirit as it is presented here in this divine word of appeal, exhortation, and implied promise. The apostle in effect calls upon the believer to 'yield himself unto God' the Holy Ghost (Rom. 6:13) as to a power and presence already dwelling in living reality within him, but waiting, as it were, for the welcome of the soul to come forth from within and take entire possession of the whole circle and range of life. It is no invitation to a spasmodic or tempestuous enthusiasm. It is a call to let the water from the mountain-springs of God rise in the man, in his purposes, in his affections, in his works, in his will, calmly and surely towards its blessed level.

Let us not forget the holy reality under its sacred imagery. This appeal of the Spirit by Paul is sent straight to the innermost heart of my reader, and of myself. What does it mean in our life, as that life is to be lived this day? By grace we believe in the Son of God revealed. Therefore most surely the Spirit is in us, for without his working we should never have 'called Jesus Lord' (1 Cor. 12:3). But are we filled, nay are we filling, with the Spirit? Is his blessed power upon our 'first springs of thought and will' a power fully welcomed there? Are we watching and praying over the matter, and humbly resolved, looking up for light, that nothing we know of in act or habit, in occupation, in recreation, in thought and word about our neighbour, in use of time or means, is such as to obstruct the rise of his 'calm excess' through all we are and all we have? Paul calls us to this humble and holy watching and resolve; and assuredly the whole Word of God promises a blissful result, to the glory not of ourselves but of our Lord, upon our so doing in his name.

So let us do then, in the name of Jesus Christ. As I said, this precept implies a promise. And the promise is unto not great or exceptional Christians, but to the Christian – who yields himself to God. At Ephesus, it was meant for the everyday Christian believer; husband, wife, parent, child, master, slave. They were all meant to live lives divinely full, from within;

'Not roughened by those cataracts and breaks
Which humour interposed so often makes';

and which are made indeed by anything and everything in
which the soul at all rebels against the Holy Ghost; but
equal, equable, under the welcomed power of the Lord.
And what this precept meant at Ephesus it means in
England, it means to the man who writes these words in
his study at Cambridge, and to his brother in Christ who
reads them wherever God has bid him dwell.

Are our lives 'full' with the fulness of multiplied duties,
of heavy calls upon every hour? Let us calm them and
illuminate them with this other fulness in its divine
simplicity. Let the Spirit, the life-giver, the revealer of
Christ, the imparter of Christ to us, have his way, and rise
and fill the man. Then the life full of toil will be a life full
also of internal peace.

The baptism of the Spirit
It will be in place here to remark on the phrase *the baptism
of the Spirit*. That phrase is not precisely Pauline. We have
only an approach to it in the words, 'by one Spirit we
were all baptized into one body' (1 Cor. 12:13). But its
connection with the subject of the fulness of the Spirit, as
seen in the Ephesian Epistle, is close and important. It
occurs in each of the Gospels and twice in the Acts (Matt.
3:11; Mark 1:8; Luke 3:16; John 1:26, 33; Acts 1:5; 11:16).
It will be seen that the Lord Jesus appears there always as
the Baptizer. And it will be seen also that while the
mentions of the holy filling are frequent, the recorded
occasions of the baptism are two only: the Day of
Pentecost, and the closely parallel occasion when in the

house of Cornelius Peter, the apostle of Pentecost, was permitted solemnly and for ever to 'open the door of faith to the Gentiles' (see Acts 11:15, 16). Nowhere in the Epistles does the precise phrase 'baptism of the Spirit' occur. Are we not thus led to the conclusion that the baptism is not to be identified with the filling, and is not, like the filling, presented to us as a blessing for which the Christian is to seek?

I am aware that the question is not without its special difficulties. The analogy of the sacrament of baptism would in itself lead us to connect the baptism of the Spirit rather with the beginning of the new life than with a great development of it; but we can hardly do this without reserve, in view of the fact that the apostles themselves were not till the Day of Pentecost, subjects of this baptism. Still, both the Pentecost and the Visit to Cornelius were not only historical events but great representative occasions, each of which was, as it were, a birth-time of the true church by the power of the Spirit. And each day may thus be held to typify and signify on a great scale the true birth-process and birth-time, by the same power, in the case of the individual soul. Anywise it is remarkable and significant that the developed teaching of the Epistles contains no appeal to the man already in Christ to seek the baptism of the Spirit. We are to be filled, and to be full of him, as those who have already received him 'from the height that knows no measure'.

In view of these facts of Scripture may I say, with tenderness and deep spiritual sympathy, that a mistake seems to underlie the practice, not uncommon now among earnest Christians, of *waiting* for a special 'baptism of the Spirit' in order to more effectual service for the Lord?

Surely, 'by one Spirit *we have been baptized* into one body' (1 Cor. 12:13). And now our part is to open in humblest faith all the avenues and regions of the soul and of the life, that we may be filled with what we already have.

And how shall this be done? Paul gives the answer: 'That we might receive the promise of the Spirit *through faith*' (Gal. 3:14). Yes, through faith, the mouth of the inner man, 'opened' that he who has promised may 'fill' it. In this brief loving appeal to the Ephesian saints, the apostle does but ask them to open and receive; to take their stand upon a promise. Not by mighty spiritual effort but in order to it is that 'promise' to be 'received'. We are to take the Lord at his word, to trust him to bless us fully in his keeping his word. We are to open to him all the inner doors of the soul, the chamber doors, as we have opened the main portal. And we are to use the same key, 'the key of promise', which is, from the other point of view, the key of our simplest and most confiding faith.

Believing, we receive. And blessed then will be the manifestations of the holy Gift received, in one special direction and another. We shall know something of what it is to be 'filled with all joy and peace in believing, that we may abound in hope, by the power of the Holy Ghost' (Rom. 15:13). We shall be on our way to be 'filled with the fruit of righteousness' (Phil. 1:11); 'filled with the knowledge of his will' (Col. 1:9). We shall be realizing something indeed, by the power of him who is the bond betwixt us and our Head, of that filling which we already possess (but possession is not realization) in him in whom 'all the fulness dwells'. Yes, we shall be filled, we shall be filling, in our finite receptivity, (Col. 1:29 with 2:10) with that 'fulness of God' (Eph. 3:19) which means whatsoever being glory in him is capable of becoming grace in us.

Here will be a blessed and continuous answer to the prayer of our Communion Service, that wonderful and pregnant petition: 'We humbly beseech thee that all we, who are partakers of this holy Communion, may be *fulfilled* with thy grace and heavenly benediction.'

Let us not forget the words which, with profound significance, just precede that prayer: 'Here we offer and present unto thee, O Lord, ourselves, our souls and bodies, to be a reasonable, holy and lively sacrifice unto thee.' We yield ourselves to him for his will. He meets us with his sacred fulness.

To this same range of truth we may refer the language of Paul about the *sealing by the Spirit*, and the *earnest of the Spirit*, and the *firstfruits of the Spirit* (Eph. 1:13, 14; 4:30; 2 Cor. 1:22; Rom. 8:23). No doubt the 'Gifts' of the primeval church are considerably in view in each of those phrases. But surely the same reasons which have constrained us to apply the apostle's language about the fulness to the 'more excellent way' of the divine life of faith, hope, and love apply here. The believer, already a believer by the Spirit's lifegiving operation, is now also 'sealed' as the property of his Master by the same Spirit's developed possession of him. And this possession, with its holy fruit, is the 'earnest' of his full possession of his God for ever in eternity; the 'first-fruits' of the harvest of 'life everlasting' which is to be reaped 'of the Spirit' then at length (Gal. 6:8).

Come forth, then eternal Spirit, and be ever coming forth, from thy secret place within our spirit, into all that we are, and all that we have, to fill all in all in us, and to overflow through us. Fill thou us in a blessed continuousness and habit, enabling us in humble continuousness to receive thee, day by day and hour by hour, through faith. At each crisis of need fill us with thy special fulness out of thy habitual. And when the hour of death shall come, so fill us that we may see with our spirit's eyes, in thy light, heaven opened, and the Son of Man standing at the right hand of God. Amen.

Chapter 12

The Holy Spirit Strengthening

For the main theme of our enquiry in the last chapter we went to the Epistle to the Ephesians. And now, for the last of our successive explorations of this continent of living truth, we come to the same Epistle again, and to a passage more full if possible than even that other of the inmost treasures of the doctrine of the Spirit.

Who has not read and re-read the closing verses of the third chapter of the Ephesians with the feeling of one permitted to look through parted curtains into the holiest place of the Christian life? Who has not longed to step into that sanctuary in a personal experience of its riches and blessings? Who that in any true sense has entered in by grace does not feel, does not know, that indeed it is rest and joy beyond all exposition to be there? It is the spiritual *summum bonum* of the pilgrimage. It is the beginning of the happiness of the eternal country.

Approaching this very sacred passage for some special meditations on one glorious part of it, let us first briefly recall its contents as a whole.

It forms the resumption of a dropped subject. At the close of Chapter 2 the apostle had written of the building of the great spiritual Temple, the true church of God, the holy structure in which every stone is living and in living contact with the *Angulare Fundamentum,* the Stone of the Corner. That structure he had described as rising, growing,

'into the holy sanctuary in the Lord'; preparing for the
eternal day of its final consecration, when it should be
ready at length and for ever to be the 'abiding habitation
of God in the Spirit' (Eph. 2:22). Then followed a long
and memorable digression, in which the imagery of
sanctuary and habitation disappears. But at the fourteenth
verse of the next chapter, our present chapter, it comes up
again. We read again, and in a like connection with the
work and grace of Father, Son, and Holy Ghost, of a
'permanent inhabitation'.[1] We see again a divine indweller,
abiding in a shrine constructed as it were of human
materials and prepared for his presence by the skill and
power of the Spirit. But there is a difference.

The former passage had to do rather with the believing
company as such, the temple of the true church. This has
to do rather with that company as seen in its individuals;
it speaks of the *hearts* of the saints (Eph. 3:17), a word
full of the thought of separate personalities; it contemplates
them as each an abode for the divine indwelling. Each
living stone is as it were taken by itself, and seen as a
miniature of the living temple; not so that the glorious
total is forgotten, for it appears throughout the whole
passage in the use of the plural ('your *hearts*', and 'with
all saints' [Eph. 3:18]), but so that the individual aspect
of the matter is the most prominent for the time. This form
of the divine inhabiting Paul here dwells upon, and
supplicates the Father of the great family (Eph. 3:15) that
by the Spirit it may take place fully and decisively in each
Ephesian disciple. And then he proceeds to prayer on
prayer, all springing from this same root of blessing (Eph.
3:17-21). He asks that the saints, thus each possessed by

---

1. The κατοικιησαι of 3:17 takes up the κατοικητηπιον of 2:22.

Christ as perpetual inhabitant, 'rooted and grounded' in that eternal love which is manifested and conveyed through him, may all together in some sort grasp the measureless dimensions of that love, and all get a new and blissful knowledge in particular of the love of Christ himself, and all be filled with 'the fulness of God', with 'the plenitude of those blessings which the infinite One is willing and able to bestow at each moment upon the finite recipient'. Then follows the great doxology in which 'glory is given', now and in the endless prospect, to the Father of the Son and of the saints in him, in view of his almighty and unmeasured power to bless, and of the coming eternal manifestation of his praise 'in the church, and in Christ Jesus'.[2]

We have thus in some slight sense transversed the paragraph and reviewed its outline. I do so partly because there is a sort of sacred necessity to do so; to be so near such treasures of revealed grace and life, and to say nothing about the rest of them because our precise concern is with only one or two, is at least difficult. But also this view of the passage as a whole brings out what I would wish to remember throughout our present enquiry, that the profoundly individual blessing and experience with which we are specially concerned is set forth in connection with more than individual interests. It is a thing which does not terminate in the saint; it goes out through him to 'all the saints', and it finds its rest and goal in the glory of God.

But now to come to the treasures of truth which are our immediate subject. They are, the Dwelling of Christ in the heart by faith, and the connection of this great gift of grace with a special work of the *Holy Spirit*.

Let me speak very simply, and at no great length, of the inhabitation of the Lord in the heart. The theme is one rather for believing and adoring prayer, and reception, and experience, than for much explanation or disquisition. A few great points stand out however so clearly from the words that I may reverently say a little of them, as in the presence of our Lord the indweller.

First, we plainly have here a truth more special than the underlying truth that 'in' every true believer Christ is, by the Holy Spirit. Precious beyond all estimate is that truth, and happy the man who habitually remembers it and acts upon it. Yes; 'Jesus Christ is in you, except ye be counterfeits' (2 Cor. 13:5); and great indeed are the inferences meant to flow direct from that fact into the Christian faith and life. But there is something more special here. For these Ephesians are addressed as no counterfeits in spiritual life; and yet Paul prays that Christ may dwell in their hearts.

Secondly, the kind of speciality is indicated by the word 'your *hearts*'; not your nature, your being, but your hearts. And 'the heart' is a word which, in Scripture, means very much the organ of the whole inner consciousness, of living thought, affection, will. Accordingly the indwelling here must be something appropriate to that organ; a blessed presence of the Lord in the saint's recollection, and love, and purposes. 'In' the Christian off his guard the Lord still 'is', in his patient mercy; but not 'dwelling in his heart'. To borrow the imagery of a Puritan commentator on the Ephesian Epistle, Christ may be present in the temple, in the church, of the believer's being, while yet he is not sitting enthroned in its choir.

Thirdly, the words of the apostle assure us that it is the

plan and purpose of the gospel that such a session of Christ in the sanctuary of affections and will should be the experience, and the abiding experience, of every disciple. Not *some* of the Ephesian saints but *all* of them are contemplated in this great prayer; in each heart of all the company Christ is thus to abide. No esoteric privilege, to be won by special achievements, or by special austerities, or under exceptional surroundings, is here in view. The means of attainment, or rather of reception, are divinely simple, as we shall presently see; this sacred bliss of the presence is to be entered upon 'by faith'. And it is meant to be not an intermittent and precarious glory, dropped for a season through the rolling clouds of doubt and fear, and soon to fade again into twilight. The word ($\kappa\alpha\tau o\iota\kappa\epsilon\iota\nu$) selected to describe it is a word made expressly to denote residence as against lodging, the abode of a master within his own home as against the turning 'aside for a night' (Jer. 14:8) of the wayfarer who will be gone tomorrow. Holy and welcome intimation! It is within the scope of prayer, and of humblest expectation, and of believing reception, that this most sacred presence of our Lord, in a mode which affects the inmost experience of his servant, shall be as continuous and as regular (may I not venture to say?) as the very consciousness of our own personality. 'Even so, come, Lord Jesus.'

Lastly, the grammatical shape here of this same verb, its aorist tense ($\kappa\alpha\tau o\iota\kappa\eta\sigma\alpha\iota$), suggests to the reader the thought not only of a divine indwelling in the heart, but of a certain *coming in* of the indweller, a *taking up* of his holy residence within. It conveys the idea of an initial entrance in order to a stated permanency of presence. And the enquiry presents itself, whether this teaches us that for each Christian, in the law of his spiritual life, there is intended to take place at some stage of his progress a definite and solemn step from a lower to a higher experience, from an ordinary to an extraordinary state of communion with his Lord.

Did Paul view the Ephesians as all then occupying a lower level from which they were to rise decisively and forthwith to another as yet unknown to them? I cannot think that his meaning can be put precisely thus, in view of the whole context, and of his whole teaching. I do not trace in the New Testament at large any formed and deliberate doctrine of such a single and ruling crisis as divinely intended in every case of life and faith, and accordingly to be sought by every convert. The blessing indicated has nothing in it to forbid that it should coincide with the earliest living acceptance of Christ by the awakened man; and it has nothing in it to forbid the belief that in countless instances it should be truly present while yet its arrival, its development, was unnoticed by the man and took place through a process which he cannot even seem to analyse.

Let no Christian judge another in this matter. But then let no Christian whose record is thus *uniformitarian* (if we may borrow a word from the geologist) think that for his friend or brother there cannot be a critical and decisive experience of the indweller's 'arrival to reside in the heart'. Testimonies innumerable, and given by gravest witnesses, tell us that such experienced arrivals of Jesus Christ there are, followed by a residence in the heart which is indeed a new and blissful experience to the man, as he discovers that what has before been an occasional and exceptional communion of soul with his living and present Redeemer may be, and in fact proves to be, prevailing and habitual. Such cases Paul, I doubt not, contemplates here, assured that within the large community at Ephesus there were many for whom such a crisis was the great spiritual need. And he includes the whole company in his prayer; partly, if I read him aright, to remind each disciple that whatever might be his experience of the arrival there was no man who might not possess, and out not to possess, the experience of the presence; but partly for another reason.

The holy reality, in this as in other things of the soul, inevitably transcended any single metaphor of it. Arrival and residence were ideas not narrowly to be limited to any one crisis of the life of faith, however great and memorable. Even for the most fully experienced, each access of conscious knowledge of the power of that presence in the heart would be, as it were, a new arrival for another stay. Such is he of whom the writer speaks, and such is his indwelling, that in the very heart itself, in the very same heart, he may from one point of view be lastingly present while from another point of view he may be arriving even now. 'Even so come, Lord Jesus.'

But while we thus speak of this sacred indwelling, this dear inner secret of the Christian life, are we forgetting our true theme, the work of the Holy Spirit? No, we are not. I have dwelt thus far upon verse 17 in order to put with the more emphasis the truth of verse 16, the revealed action of the Spirit in this matter.

Observe then that it is *he* who so to speak stands behind this whole wonderful experience as its immediate agent and secret. The apostle bows his knees to the Father that these dear Ephesians, each and all, one by one, may be dealt with in divine speciality by the Holy Ghost. He must act in them and through them if Christ is thus to dwell within. Deep below the Christian's consciousness, within those springs of thought and will which are such mysteries to the person himself, the Spirit of the Father – and of the Son – must do the work of 'strengthening with might in the inner man'. Operating there with the divine skill which violates nothing in the nature he has made, and with the divine power which can do what he will in and with that nature. He must give, he will give, supernaturally to the man's inmost self a spiritual firmness and vigour which shall discard certain deep fears and do certain acts that could not otherwise be done.

Sacredly significant indeed is the phraseology. In order to a reception into me of what is altogether the gift of God and not the sequel or remuneration of any toils or endurances of mine, I yet need to be 'strengthened with might by the Spirit in' ('*deep* within', as the Greek, $\epsilon\iota\varsigma$ $\tau o\nu$ $\H{\epsilon}\sigma\omega$ $\mathring{\alpha}\nu\theta\rho\omega\pi o\nu$, seems precisely to indicate) 'the inner man'. And I ask what this means, what is the occasion in this matter for a divine *strengthening,* where perhaps I might have looked rather for such words as subduing or alluring. And I read the answer in the light of the truth that the blessing in question is the residence always in the heart of its *Master* and *Lord*, who where he dwells must rule; who enters not to cheer and soothe alone but before all things else to reign. And I remember that nature, nature in the Fall, does not like that presence in that aspect; fears greatly to admit 'this Man to reign over us' (Luke 19:14). I remember that the regenerate soul itself – such is the dimness of sight and the spiritual imbecility of even the child of God 'in this tabernacle' – all too easily loses its conscious certainties of the absolute tenderness along with

the absolute sovereignty and royalty of the Lord who
'stands at the' inner 'door and knocks' (Rev. 3:20); it
trembles lest his incoming should of necessity bring some
nameless shock or sorrow in its train. 'I dreaded to yield
myself without reserve to Jesus Christ,' said a Christian
kinswoman of my own, relating to a little circle the story
of her own experience; 'I felt so sure that he would take
from me my little Hugh.' But the strength of a quiet
confidence in the perfect wisdom and love of the claimant
King, along with a calm intuition into his adorable beauty
and desirableness, at length overcame that dread; and the
door was opened, cost what it might. He has come in –
and the child has not been taken from the mother's
embrace, or rather it has been given back to her, 'Isaac-
like', more than ever her own, out of that supreme
surrender.

Do we not understand in the light of such an instance
the need of the Holy Spirit's *strength-giving* work, in order
to the reception of the Lord Christ as the abiding and ruling
inhabitant of the very heart? And do we not see how it is
the special function of none other than *the Spirit* so to
deal with the inner man? He is the Glorifier of Christ; it is
his, we have seen above, to –

'Show us that loving Man
   That rules the courts of bliss,
The Lord of hosts, the mighty God,
   The eternal Prince of Peace.'

And in the sacred matter of the indwelling, it is he
accordingly who so 'shows' him to the wistful soul that it
sees, with an intuition truly its own yet supernatural in its

conditions, how safe, how satisfying, how blissful is his all-ruling presence, not only in 'the courts of bliss' but in the believing sinner's heart. So the door is opened, for this private but royal entrance of the King of Glory. So work thou then in us all, O Spirit of the Father and of the Son.

And here, as our meditation on this bright oracle closes, let us lastly remember those words of verse 17; *by faith*. They are all-important to a practical use of the truth and promise of our Lord's indwelling. On the one hand they remind us that, if that indwelling is to be our experience indeed, there is need of genuine personal action on the Christian's own part, action God-taught and God-granted, as we have seen, yet not the less the man's own. The Lord 'stands at the door and knocks' (Rev. 3:20); the man, the inner man, must rise and set it open. Faith is the act of man though it is 'the gift of God'; and 'by means of faith' (Eph. 2:8) Christ arrives in the heart to dwell there. But on the other hand, because the action of the soul *is* in this case faith, and nothing else, the words remind us for our 'comfort and good hope' that the action is in effect nothing but the utmost simplicity of reception. Do we need to define 'faith' to ourselves over again? Has not every instance of the use of the word by our Lord himself in the Gospels long ago assured us that it means just personal reliance, personal trust, personal entrustment? It is the open arms which in their emptiness embrace Christ, the open lips which receive him as the bread of the soul, the life, the all. As in justification so in this glorious sequel, our part is to take the promise as it stands, to take the thing in the envelope of the promise, and to act upon its holy presence and reality.

And he who is 'the Spirit of faith' (2 Cor. 4:13) is faith's appropriate giver, for this as for all things. For this, as for our earliest acts of trust, he enables us, by manifesting Christ in his divine trustworthiness and putting the soul in contact with him, the seen, the trusted, the welcomed Lord.

'O Son of God, who lovest me,
    I will be thine alone;
And all I have, and all I am,
    Shall henceforth be thine own.'

It is a 'full and glad surrender'. 'And all this hath worked that one and the self-same *Spirit*.'

Our enquiries and meditations on the person and the work of the Holy Spirit here draw to a close. It is needless to spend words in owning how fragmentary, how imperfect, even on a very modest standard, the attempt has been. But I can hope and can pray that my reader may have gained here and there a suggestion, perhaps about some forgotten side of a familiar truth, and that he may have felt some stimulus to an ever-deepening search into the divine Word for more and yet more of the treasures of the truth and of the Holy Spirit.

And may writer and reader both be found, through his great grace, among the happy ones who, living by the Spirit, walk by the Spirit, and by the Spirit draw continually out of the fulness of Jesus Christ, to whom by the Spirit they are conjoined in an unspeakable union.

More than thirty years ago that great man, great thinker and preacher, and great saint, Adolphe Monod, lay on his sorely suffering and comparatively early deathbed at Paris. Led in his youth through experiences of complicated doubt and profound melancholy to the foot of the atoning cross of a divine and personal Redeemer, and to the solemn and glad experiences of the work of the Spirit in the believer's life, and to a holy submission and repose before the whole revealed truth of our salvation by grace, he had spent his years and used all his great gifts of intellect and of heart 'in the defence and confirmation of the gospel', with the one longing, loving desire to bring others into the peace and certainty he had found, and to build them up in it. Now he was dying, at the age of fifty-four. His beloved ministry was over, and he was looking back on work and onward into the heavenly rest from his Pisgah-top of suffering. One day, in the midst of much physical distress, a few words escaped him, his brief summary of a Christian's peace, strength, aim, and all. I close by repeating them, and invite my reader with me to make them the motto not only of death hereafter but of our life this day :

**'ALL IN CHRIST;
BY THE HOLY SPIRIT;
FOR THE GLORY OF GOD.
ALL ELSE IS NOTHING.'**

In 1881, Handley Moule (1841-1920) became the first principal of Ridley Hall Theological College, Cambridge and in 1899 Norrisian professor of divinity. In 1901 he became Bishop of Durham. In addition to this volume on the Holy Spirit, he wrote expositions and commentaries on the New Testament epistles, as well as devotional books. Christian Focus also publishes Moule's biography of Charles Simeon.